THE METAMORPHOSIS OF BAUBO

The Metamorphosis of

BAUBO

Myths of Woman's Sexual Energy

WINIFRED MILIUS LUBELL

Vanderbilt University Press NASHVILLE & LONDON

First Edition 1994

94 95 96 97 98 99   5 4 3 2 1

This publication is made from recycled
paper and meets the minimum requirements
of American National Standard for
Information Sciences—Permanence of Paper
for Printed Library Materials. ⊗

Library of Congress Cataloging-in-
Publication Data
Winifred Milius Lubel, 1914–
The metamorphosis of Baubo: myths of
woman's sexual energy / Winifred Milius
Lubell
p. cm.
Includes bibliographical references and
index.
ISBN 0-8265-1251-8 (alk. paper) —
ISBN 0-8265-1252-6 (pbk. : alk. paper)
1. Women, Prehistoric.   2. Art, Prehistoric.
3. Women in art.   4. Sexuality in art.
5. Fertility cults.   6. Art, Greek.
7. Mythology, Greek.   I. Title.
GN799.W66L83 1994   93-42729
305.4—dc20   CIP

Manufactured in the United States of
America

Waters of the sacred rivers are flowing backward.

Justice, order, all things are turned about.

The plans of men are full of deceit and their oaths,

sacred to the Gods, are no longer fixed in place.

Stories will turn my life so that it has a good reputation.

Honor is returning to womankind,

and the old discordant tales about women

will no longer be recounted.

The ancient minstrels of the Muses shall cease to sing

those songs of our faithlessness.

Would that Phoebus, Lord of Music, had granted us

the inspired gift of the lyre, so that we might

reply with an ode about the tribe of men.

For the long years have as much to tell

about the fate of women as of men.

—Euripides, Medea, ll. 410–30

Translated by Winifred Milius Lubell

CONTENTS

List of Illustrations, ix

Foreword by Marija Gimbutas, xiii

Preface, xv

Acknowledgments, xxi

1 *Uncovering the Rubble, 1*

2 *Sage Iambe and Raucous Baubo, 13*

3 *Baubo Verified, 21*

4 *Festival Sacrament, Sacred Laughter, 29*

5 *Baubo and the Scholars, 44*

6 *The Image Defined, 55*

7 *Sacred or Profane? 84*

8 *Metamorphosis to Monster, 98*

9 *The Transformer Transformed, 114*

10 *Baubo Meets Her Dark Sisters, 130*

11 *The She and the He of It, 147*

Appendix 1
Homeric *Hymn to Demeter* (Synopsis), 161

Appendix 2
A Selection of Myths Reflecting the Spirit of Baubo, 166

Notes, 187

Bibliography, 201

Index, 209

ILLUSTRATIONS

All illustrations are by Winifred Milius Lubell, unless otherwise noted. Captions accompanying illustrations include source information in parentheses. When two or more sources are given, the illustration has been composed from elements of each. See Bibliography for full titles and details of publications cited as sources.

0.1   Babylonian goddess squatting, xv

0.2   Mayauel, Aztec goddess of pulque and childbirth, xviii

1.1   A vision of Baubo dancing, 2

1.2   An imaginary moon-blood ritual, 6

1.3   Dancing women and symbolic vulvas, 7

1.4   Hellenistic statuette of Baubo/Isis, 9

1.5   A young girl's puberty celebration, 10

2.1   Persephone vanishing into Hades, 15

2.2   Iambe offering the *kykeon* to Demeter, 19

3.1   The Sumerian goddess Bau, 23

3.2   A Sumerian goddess of fertility and fecundity, 25

3.3   An Egyptian musical celebration, 27

4.1   Plaque honoring Demeter and Persephone, 32

4.2   The *ana-suromai* of Baubo, 35

6.1   The dancing "Venus" of Galgenberg, 56

6.2   Paleolithic images of the vulva, 58

6.3   Bolivian vulva carvings on boulders, 60

6.4   Female figures from the cave of Angles-sur-l'Anglin, 62

6.5   The Woman of Le Gabillou, 63

6.6   Carved and inscribed reindeer bone from Le Placard, 64

6.7   The "Shameless Venus" of Laugerie Basse, 66

6.8   The "Venus" of Laussel, 68

6.9   Figurine from Kostenki, Russia, 69

6.10 Figurine from Lespugue, France, 71

6.11 Photograph of Lespugue figurine, 72

6.12 Photograph of the "Fish Goddess" of Lepenski Vir, 74

6.13 Carved sandstone boulders from Lepenski Vir, 75

6.14 Bone figurine from Beersheba, 77

6.15 Phoenician terra-cotta, 78

6.16 Gold amulet from Tel Baiteglain, 79

6.17 Cycladic marble torso and head, 80

6.18 Marble statue from Delos, 81

6.19 "My Lady of M'alta," 82

7.1   Cliff engraving of an ostrich hunt from the Sahara, 85

7.2   A Sumerian goddess of beasts, birds, and fish, 86

7.3   Babylonian cylinder seal from Ur, 88

7.4   A birthing scene of the Mimbres people, 89

7.5   Woman in the form of a frog, 90

7.6   Frog from the Minoan palace of Phaistos, 92

7.7   Anasazi frog shell pendant from Colorado, 93

7.8   Young woman in frog posture of birthing, 94

7.9   Egyptian "magic" knife with Heket, the Frog Goddess, 95

8.1   Demeter and Persephone, 99

8.2   Seven Priene statuettes of Baubo, 100

8.3   Photograph of a Priene Baubo, 102

8.4   The Gorgons, sisters of Medusa, 106

8.5   Perseus slaying Medusa, 107

8.6   Athena wearing her Medusa Aegis, 109

8.7   Gorgon/Medusa figure from Melos, 111

8.8   A winged Medusa, 112

9.1   Three "Baubo" dancers, 116

9.2   Terra-cotta statues of Baubo/Isis, 118

9.3   Isis seated upon a harvest basket, 119

9.4   Baubo upon a sow, 121

9.5   Women worshipping the sacred bull Apis, 124

9.6   Medusa and the Evil Eye, 126

9.7   Hellenistic terra-cotta figure, 127

9.8   Terra-cotta Baubo with the Eye symbol, 128

10.1   Gorgon-like figure with winged lions, 132

10.2   Double-tailed mermaid from the cathedral of
       Saint Michael, Lucca, Italy, 133

10.3   A double-tailed Spanish mermaid, 134

10.4   La Potta di Modena, 136

10.5   The Whore and the Beast, 137

10.6   Ethiopian magic scroll, 138

10.7   Sheilah-Na-Gig from Kelpeck Church, Herefordshire, 140

10.8   Sheilah-Na-Gig from County Cavan, Ireland, 142

10.9   A medieval witch, 145

11.1   A garlanded herm statue, 149

11.2   A phallus-bird nesting over vulva eggs, 154

11.3   Sheilah-Na-Gig kissed by a "man-animal", 155

11.4   The Divine Yoni, 156

11.5   The Devi, Goddess Ardhanarîsvara, 158

A1.1   Persephone abducted by Hades, 161

A2.1   Three Gorgon-Baubos, 166

FOREWORD

As a single small potsherd can make it possible to reconstruct a large vase, so also a single and seemingly insignificant ancient poetic episode can provide a missing link for reconstructing an important mythical personage and her meaning. Such is the case with Baubo, a nurse mentioned in the Homeric *Hymn to Demeter*, in a few passages from Orphic literature, and in later commentaries on the religious rites practiced at Eleusis. Winifred Lubell's painstaking detective work finally provides us with a fuller understanding of this important but little-known deity, who has touched the human psyche for millennia.

From only the briefest literary record of Baubo's comforting jokes and skirt-raising gesture (*ana-suromai*), Lubell ingeniously builds a comprehensive comparative study. This investigation spans from the Paleolithic through the Middle Ages in time, and from Europe and Egypt through Siberia to the Americas in breadth. Lubell relates Baubo's skirt-raising, vulva-exposing gesture to a host of extremely old carved, sculpted, and painted forms, including the nearly ubiquitous frog-shaped images, not only from early Egyptian culture but also from much earlier European and Anatolian periods. These ancient images, brought so powerfully to these pages by Lubell's drawings, have always communicated strong female energies that have defied annihilation, even with the introduction of new religions and the scrutiny of the medieval Inquisition. Indeed, as Lubell illustrates, we find the same Baubo-related frog-like female form with exposed vulva—the mysterious Sheila-Na-Gig—carved into the walls of Irish and English churches of the twelfth through the sixteenth centuries.

Baubo and the frog goddess exude an essence that lingers from sacred fertility rituals, from a time when agriculture still bound and defined ancient cultures. These images certainly are not pornographic but rather express persistent awe of female sexual and procreative energies. Baubo's strangeness to modern eyes warns of the danger of her loss, but as Winifred Lubell demonstrates, Baubo is a true survivor, and her power is yet strong.

Marija Gimbutas

PREFACE

It began for me with a gesture, the gesture of a woman seen in various drawings, reliefs, and figurines whose squatting pose emphasized her pudenda (see fig. 0.1). As an artist and book illustrator, with a special interest in mythology, I began to collect and draw these images in my sketchbooks, finding them again and again in museums, in books on primitive art, and in works on Paleolithic art. The gesture repeatedly appeared to me in the iconography of cultures throughout the world. I found them puzzling, disturbing, and beautiful, even before I came to grips with the questions of their meaning.

Somewhat later, I discovered that the Greeks had a way of designating a similar gesture; they used a word that means simply to lift up one's clothes. In classical antiquity that provocative gesture was frequently linked to an odd servant-nurse personage known as Baubo, alias Iambe. I found one version of Iambe/Baubo in an ancient poem called the *Hymn to Demeter*, where she performs a small but pivotal role in the tale of Persephone and Demeter. Evidence in that poem and other sources suggests that this character may have played a more significant part in sacred fertility rituals associated with Demeter and performed at the Attic festivals of Thesmo-

FIGURE 0.1 *Babylonian cylinder seal from Ur, showing a goddess squatting. Ca. 1500* BCE
(Devereux, 1983, p. 41.)

phoria and the Eleusinian Mysteries. I was soon scanning scholarly journals and books, turning first to the index, hunting for any mention of Iambe or Baubo. Many signposts indicated that others had preceded me; clues had been dropped along the way by Jane Harrison, Charles Picard, Jean Claire, Maurice Olender, Walter Burkert, and others.

This book grew from my need to comprehend the role of the old nurse Baubo, her gesture, her jokes, her so-called obscenity, and her aberrant behavior. It has sometimes been difficult to decide whether she stood among the Olympians or was mortal; whether she was a fertility metaphor, a symbol of the Evil Eye, or an iconograph left over from the prehistoric world. At times, she seemed a very real person standing there next to me, while at other times only a faint echo of her mockery remained in the air.

I began to see that over millennia the imagery surrounding Baubo assumed many deviant and startling forms, which in Judeo-Christian times were replaced, muted, or transformed into the shapes of demons, grotesqueries, and witches. Baubo's spirit is traceable in the forms of Medusa, in many mermaid images, and in the strange sculptures called Sheilah-Na-Gigs, which are found in a number of medieval churches in Ireland, Wales, and England. The narrative of her story can be tracked in etymology, in historical references, and in myths all over the world. But always Baubo's graphic gesture of exposure kept me searching, while providing me with more and more insight into the transmutations of this complex and enigmatic figure.

For more than ten years prior to my initial confrontation with Baubo, I was deeply immersed in studying whatever images of Paleolithic and Neolithic art I could find. The work of Marija Gimbutas opened windows for me, as did the books of Henri Delporte, Alexander Marshack, and Jacquetta Hawkes. The study of their work and my own search for the compelling images that I continued to find in museums and in the photographic record began to yield results in my own creative activity. I produced a large body of graphic work—drawings, wood engravings, color woodcuts, and collages—all inspired by those mythological feminine images.

In 1986, at my first exhibition of this new graphic work, I found an eager and receptive audience. I quickly became aware, however, that these images, though anchored in the historical and archeological record, were outside the cultural experience of my audience; they were strange to people in a way that worked against my purpose. It was clear that even the most visually sophisticated needed help in absorbing these potent and long-forgotten feminine images. Some few might recognize the twenty-thousand-year-old "Venus" of Laussel figure (see chap. 6, fig. 8), but most of my audience had limited access to the many hundreds of ancient female images that are now becoming part of our artistic heritage. Few understood the complexity of these figures or knew of their vast geographical range, extending from Siberia to Spain; few knew that these same symbolic concepts also exist in non-European cultures; even fewer were aware of how ancient these figures are or how recently most have been unearthed. Because written explanations were clearly needed to accompany all this unfamiliar material, I began preparing commentaries for my subsequent exhibits. This book is, in some ways, a development from that early effort to introduce to my viewing audience the images I now associate with the spirit of Baubo.

Working on this book, I have become uneasy with the casual and arbitrary identifications of "Venus" and "fertility goddess" for these figures. In our Western cultural heritage, the title "Venus" presumes a specific kind of sexual identity that I find at odds with the spirit of Baubo. Venus, a Roman deity, was the alter ego of the Greek goddess Aphrodite. Both were loved and feared for a species of sexual power defined from a male point of view. The title "goddess" signifies a non-mortal, usually a consort of a god, a female whose power is god-given. Even the power of Athena, that assertive protector of Attic Athens, was contrived, created, and controlled by Zeus. Her armor—helmet, spear, and shield—were bestowed by Zeus. Her devastating aegis, decorated with the Medusa's head and fringed by serpents, was a potent symbol of authority. But Athena's aegis was on loan to her from her father, Zeus, while he, the Loud Thunderer, brandished his ultimate weapon of destruction, the lightning bolt. I began to understand that the effective symbol of the images I had been assembling is the innate energy of the female body and that to call such figures "Venus" or "fertility goddess" is too simplistic. Those labels reduce the significance of the body to cliché, when the figures actually have far richer symbolic implications. I came to see that Baubo's gesture was not uncommon among iconographic female images from many distant parts of the globe. I found her charac-

FIGURE O.2 *Mayauel, Aztec goddess of pulque and childbirth, shown squatting on her tortoise throne. Pre-Columbian codex preserved in* Codex Laud, *Bodleian Library, Oxford, ca. 1520.*
(Burland, 1953, pl. 14.)

teristic posture in figures from islands in the Pacific, in the art of India, China, and the Caribbean, and in pre-Columbian codices from Mexico (see fig. 0.2).

In the view of anthropologist Peggy Reeves Sanday, "Myths of former female power provide men with a rationale for segregating themselves from women and a reason for dominating 'tyrannical' women. Wherever men perceive women in such terms, it is likely that women have considerable informal power. Thus, myths of former female power mirror the paradoxical relationship between the sexes that actually exists."[1] I see Baubo as one such myth of female power. But her power was never symbolized by gleaming armor or by beauty bestowed on her by a male Olympian. Her power was that of her body. She is a symbol of the nurturing and transformative energies of women, which combine with women's resourcefulness and laughter. The spontaneity of Baubo's laughter flashes out like graffiti across the ruins of the past. Her jests have vanished, but her wry and startling gesture and the record of her comic wit remain. Many have suggested that laughter among women is the hidden side of women's sexuality. That kind of laughter—often associated with the trickster figure and with fertility—was often used in sacred and joyful ritual to ease a stressful situation, to set painful matters in perspective, to restore balance.

I think it would be a sad mistake for us to lose sight of Baubo and her icon, the vulva, to relinquish her playful joking, to let her slide out of Western consciousness into scholarly obscurity or into the netherworld of demons or pornography. Her strangeness to modern eyes warns of the danger of her loss. But Baubo is a survivor. She has consistently refused to stay put in a single or confining role of womanhood. She is irreverent—and she is sacred. She represents those revered sexual and procreative feminine energies that merge to form the nurturers, the transformers, and the balancers, without whom civilization cannot survive. Baubo's arresting gesture of exposure holds the clue to understanding all the metamorphoses of this complex and enigmatic figure. My hope is that the words and images in this book will contribute to a fuller understanding of her historical evolution and to a greater awareness of the latent power that her true sexual persona represents.

W. M. L.
Wellfleet, Massachusetts
June 1993

ACKNOWLEDGMENTS

I wish to thank the many friends who sustained me in the long process of writing this book. I owe special thanks to Kristine Rosenthal Keese, who believed from the start in the importance of Baubo; to Mary Carroll Smith, who led me into the intricacies of goddess history and imagery; to my friend the late Sophia Ames Boyer, who first introduced me to the delights of classical Greek; to Leigh Cauman, who proofread with great patience an early manuscript version; to Virginia Chapin, Ruth Hollander, Margaret Smalzel, and Hilda and Herbert Lass for their unfailing enthusiasm and support; and to Helen Barolini for telling me about the Modena image.

I also want to thank my agent, Mary Jack Wald, for her warmth and understanding, as well as for her perseverance. I am grateful to Bard Young, my editor at Vanderbilt University Press, for his sympathetic and meticulous reading. I thank Norma Holt for her photographs, and Miriam Robbins Dexter for her critical reading of an earlier version of this Baubo story. I am particularly grateful to all the staff at the Wellfleet Library. I owe special thanks to Marija Gimbutas for her encouragement and effort on my behalf.

Special thanks must go to my sons David and Stephen, who supplied me with much important source material and who helped me with the tedious details of notes and picture captions. Last and most of all I thank my husband, Cecil Lubell, who has tried to help me understand the virtues of simple prose.

CHAPTER ONE

Here are your gates of eternity, your pit, your trapdoor,

your fissure in the earth before which the priestess sways.

Here is the lair of tabu, the grove of ritual.

Here I was born.

—*Robin Morgan*[1]

Uncovering the Rubble

Baubo. Who was she? Where did she come from? What does she represent? Baubo is one of the names of a mythical Greek woman, said to be a servant or wet nurse to the grain goddess Demeter. In certain Greek religious writings and later acounts of Greek religious rites, Baubo exposes her vulva before Demeter, an act called *ana-suromai*, a Greek verb literally meaning to lift one's skirts (see fig. 1.1). The effect was to make Demeter laugh during a time when the Grain Goddess was deep in mourning over the loss of her daughter, Persephone. But Baubo can be seen as a much

FIGURE 1.1 *A vision of Baubo dancing.*
(Drawing of an original design derived from a small Greek dish.
Museum of Fine Arts, Boston, item 13.152.)

older symbol for the power and energy of female sexuality. She can also be viewed as a trickster figure, who with her own jokes, magic, and laughter embodies fecundity and fertility. We have no images of a clearly identifiable Baubo, but her various shapes and her memory have persisted in myth and ritual. She was neither goddess nor night demon, though at times she was claimed as both.

This book is my attempt to follow the twisting trail that Baubo has left for us. Because this is such an ancient trail, overlaid with taboo and obfuscation, I will rely as much on images as on written evidence to establish Baubo's identity. Although distinct forms of expression, the written record and the visual image become inseparable. Another twist in the ancient trail is around Baubo's name. Her nomenclature is confused; she has had many names, among them Iambe, Isis, and Bau. As Iambe she played a minor role as a servant or nurse to Demeter, the ancient grain goddess of the Olympian pantheon headed by Zeus. In this work I refer to her as Iambe/Baubo, rather than Bau, one of her Sumerian names, or Isis, her later Hellenistic title.

My first encounter with Baubo occurred when I chanced upon her name in Jane Ellen Harrison's *Prolegomena to the Study of Greek Religion,* an illuminating and widely known study written in 1903 and still a storehouse of insights and information. Baubo is mentioned only once in that work, on page 569, where, after an intensive discussion of Eleusinian rites, Harrison concludes, "After this is the action of Baubo."[2] She then refers the interested reader to two footnotes. Harrison deliberately leaves the first, a lengthy quotation from the Byzantine historian Michael Psellus (d. 1078 CE), in Greek. In the second, she says: "The account of Psellus is for obvious reasons rather resumed than translated. Some of the rites recorded by Psellus are not in harmony with modern conventions, and for my purpose it is not needful to discuss them. But once for all I wish to record my conviction that such evil as we find in these mysteries we bring with us. . . . The story of Babo or Baubo has always been a stumbling block."[3]

Psellus, the eleventh-century Christian historian quoted by Harrison, was keenly interested in Greek concepts of demons. In his account, he describes archaic events that he thought took place at Eleusis, an important center of Demeter worship. He wrote that a pantomime was performed by goat-legged men in the presence of Demeter and Persephone. The pantomime reenacts Zeus's rape of Demeter, in which Zeus sacrifices or exhibits the testicles of a goat, perhaps as a symbol of his power and potency. Then came the rites of Dionysus, when a sacred chest (*kista*) and a special round cake encrusted with many knobs (*popanon*) were displayed. Next came the dance of the sacred initiates named Korubas and Koures, mimicking forms of various demons. Only after this, according to Psellus, did Baubo make her entrance. "She pulled up her gown revealing her thighs and pudenda (*gunaikeios kteis*). Thus they gave her a name which covered her with shame (*aido*). In this disgraceful manner the initiation ceremonies [at Eleusis] came to an end."[4]

Psellus's version of the Eleusinian Mysteries was Harrison's "stumbling block" and the beginning of my acquaintance with Iambe/Baubo. In subsequent years, as my notes and files grew and as my questions multiplied, I tried to classify and make a meaningful pattern from the welter of esoteric bits and pieces that I was unearthing. I found myself confronted with an unfamiliar and disquieting female iconography of vulvas. As a visual artist, I responded to their energy and felt the need to accept their offerings, but many obstacles remained in the way.

In the *Encyclopedia of Religions*, Baubo is described as "associated, often confusedly, with anything obscene in the ancient world, particularly with obscene words and objects that evoke female sexuality." The article was written by the French historian Maurice Olender, who points out that there is but a single unconnected reference to Baubo in the work of the Greek philosopher Empedocles (490–430 BCE).[5] Hesychius, a fifth century CE Alexandrian author of an important Greek lexicon, claimed that Empedocles had equated Baubo, the nurse serving Demeter, with the noun *koilia* and that *koilia* also had the meaning of a body cavity, womb, or vulva.[6] Thus the first written evidence connecting Baubo with the vulva was established.

The story of Baubo as a metaphor for *koilia*, as a comic figure performing her gesture of exposure, her *ana-suromai*, does not rest solely on these accounts of Psellus and Hesychius. Other archaic sources hold stories that will be related in the chapters to follow. As we will see, the written name of Baubo appeared, but always briefly, in later Greek and Latin inscriptions, poetry, and legends, usually in connection with bawdy or aberrant behavior. Olender comments, "Baubo is difficult to trace, her trail is misty;

she exists only in those places among the whisperings of nurses, between the barking of dogs and the places of night demons, those areas where improper words and gestures are accompanied by the laughter of women."[7]

Although she is not as impalpable as all that, identifying Baubo is not a simple matter of listing chapter and verse. She resists a single identity and is not easily pinned down to a unique function. The accumulation of available source material shows her to be a complex and elusive persona who is sometimes a nurse, servant, or priestess, sometimes a participant with goddesses in the *hieros gamos* (sacred marriage) ritual of certain ancient rites. She was also referred to as *Bona Dea*, goddess of women, while others saw her role simply as bawd, night demon, or the Evil Eye. In the following pages, the idea or spirit of Baubo will be investigated beyond the limits of specific literary verifications and also beyond any single cultural context. In Olender's opinion, "Baubo was certainly associated with matters of fertility, but one cannot, as has so often been done, reduce her to this single function. More precisely, a representation of fertility is complex. It can seem to be paradoxical because it mobilizes a network of multiple images, which in some cases were connected by the Ancients with Baubo."[8]

Baubo was probably an extremely ancient aspect of certain agricultural rituals of fecundity, when specially appointed women squatted over the newly plowed fields and gave their "moon blood," their menstrual fluid, back to the earth; or of a time when priestesses may have officiated over archaic feminine puberty rites (see fig. 1.2). In the fiercely misogynist climate of later patriarchal cultures, these old, old female rituals that had been closely connected with the earth and its cycles faded away or were effectively obliterated. The concept of menstrual blood as part of earth's sacred energy no longer fit the ideology of the emerging aggressive civilizations that had seized power. Gradually, Baubo was transformed into an obscure creature of long-forgotten rituals. Her "moon blood," once understood as "wise blood" or "magic blood,"[9] became something to be feared and was rejected as an obscenity. But in her earliest forms, when Baubo as vulva was a metaphor or symbol for female sexual energy, she was never personified in terms of seduction or pleasuring. Only much later was she tinged with obscenity.

The vulva was a Paleolithic symbol of female power and regenerative energy, dating from 30,000 BCE. It remains an image that defies repressive boundaries. William Irwin Thompson observes that "this miraculous na-

FIGURE 1.2 *Moon-blood ritual.*
(Linoleum print of an original design by W. M. L.)

ture of the vulva seems to have taken hold of the imagination of Paleolithic humanity. . . . But the vulva is the magical wound that bleeds and heals itself every month, and because it bleeds in sympathy with the dark of the moon, the vulva is an expression not of physiology, but of cosmology. The moon dies and is reborn; woman bleeds but does not die, and when she does not bleed for ten lunar months, she brings forth new life. It is easy to see how Paleolithic man would be in awe of woman, and how woman's

FIGURE 1.3 *Designs such as these, of dancing women and symbolic vulvas, were inscribed in wet clay on cave walls at Pech-Merle, La Roch, Fontalés, and La Gare de Couze in France, some 20,000 years ago.*
(Drawings derived from Delporte, 1979, figs. 38, 39, 42; and Marshack, 1972, pp. 308–310.)

mysteries would be at the base of a religious cosmology."[10] This high degree of awe and commitment to an understanding of the sacredness of the female and her mysteries remained constant throughout the late Paleolithic, through the Neolithic, and into the Bronze Age. As a result of recent archaeological research, an ever-expanding treasury of available images from the Middle East, Egypt, Old Europe,[11] and the vast regions inhabited by Indo-Europeans now reinforces this view (see fig. 1.3). Out of all this richness, I have chosen only those images that seemed to me to have direct relevance to Baubo, or to the unveiling of Baubo before Demeter.

As I circled around Baubo's incarnations, I began to see that there were two forces at work: the great power and vitality of the images that I was gathering, the way that they repeated and played against each other, and the weight of the words bearing evidence of Baubo's trail. Image and word were jockeying for position, first one in ascendancy, then the other. I came to see that they were not actually in competition but that they depended on each other. My hope is that finally a balance is achieved between these two complementary components. In the first five chapters, I trace Baubo's paper trail. Though I make use of the visual component, the written history of Baubo, her archaic and convoluted tale, dominates the images. Beginning with chapter 6 the visual component becomes paramount. Here the iconography of the vulva as symbol and metaphor joins with the words of the myths, and a fuller picture of Baubo begins to emerge.

Thus, early in this quest for Baubo it became clear to me that Baubo cannot be understood as a local personality or as a unique cultural symbol. She is no more Greek than African, no more Attic than Paleolithic (see figs. 1.4 and 1.5). The image of Baubo spans eras and cuts across cultures, like a ubiquitous time-travelling pilgrim. Maurice Olender identifies two possible approaches to Baubo study:

> Either one accepts Baubo as arising from some faraway place purged of any Greek origin, which then gives one the right to take a guided tour of the whole earth, and Baubo's *ana-suromai* [her gesture of lifting her skirts] is just something done in a Greek place by a foreign servant-woman; or else Baubo is seen as a sort of turning disk, a center of various radiations inspiring general theories about agro-mystical obscenities and or magic.[12]

Olender is correct, for the two approaches do represent contrasting procedures. Many scholars prefer the second, which is anchored in the view that Baubo is best understood as an essentially Greek character whose actions must be seen exclusively in terms of the mystical rites performed at Eleusis or other Greek festivals. I find the first approach more convincing and revealing. For that reason, my emphasis will be more in line with Olender's "world tour," with the Greek Iambe/Baubo a single manifestation of a recurring symbol of female sexual energy, as a transforming and balancing force that cuts across all oceans, all boundaries.

The universality of Baubo as an embodiment of feminine sexual power is reconfirmed in myths from many parts of the world and from different

FIGURE 1.4

*Baubo/Isis. Hellenistic statue
from Alexandria, Egypt.
Second-third century* CE.
(Perdrizet, 1921, p. 55.)

FIGURE 1.5 *A young girl's puberty celebration from a rock painting. Zimbabwe, South Africa. Possibly late Paleolithic.*
(Rudner, 1970, pl. 22.)

epochs, myths that repeat in various forms the gesture of Baubo, as well as her laughter. Appendix 2 contains a Hittite myth and a Sumerian myth, two Egyptian tales, and a Japanese legend. I also include a contemporary story from the Philippines which, in its way, is a myth in the making.

There is great interest today in this kind of comparative mythology, for archaeological discoveries of the last decades have augmented and reinforced the accuracy of many myths, previously thought fanciful. The work of Marija Gimbutas in the area that she designates "Old Europe," James Mellaart's work at Çatal Hüyük in Anatolia, the discoveries at Lepenski Vir in Serbia, the continuing work in Crete, and the ongoing work of countless other scientists have given us a fresh way of surveying this vast span of time. Each year new information is uncovered about the Paleolithic and

Neolithic eras that has to be fitted into the complex puzzle of women's role in prehistory.

Feminist historians such as Gerda Lerner, Barbara G. Walker, Riane Eisler, Charlene Spretnak, Nor Hall, Eva C. Keuls, and their colleagues are opening up new vistas. Eisler uses the apt terms *gynocentric* for woman-based cultures as opposed to *androcentric*, or male-based cultures. I shall use these helpful terms in analyzing when and why the early gynocentric societies were attacked and destroyed or, at best, twisted out of recognizable shape by androcentric might.

Many attitudes have changed, as new discoveries continue to be made. Yet the old entrenched positions persist. For example, in their recent excavations at Old Corinth, archaeologists of the American School of Classical Studies at Athens have unearthed a sanctuary of Demeter and Kore (another name for Persephone) at Acrocorinth that had been used as a place of worship, with few interruptions, from the sixth century BCE until the fourth century CE. In the school's 1987 publication, *Demeter and Persephone in Ancient Corinth*, Demeter is described as one who is "capable of enjoying an earthy joke *with a nasty old crone called Baubo* [emphasis added], who had a weakness for exhibitionism."[13]

Surely this is a misreading of both Baubo and Demeter and the character of their relationship. Perhaps the old nurse, who had seen so much happen during her long life, was saying to Demeter: "Remember! Remember the way it really happened. You were raped by Zeus. You then gave birth to a girl child, who in her turn was abducted and raped by her uncle, Hades, with the connivance of Zeus; and it is Kore, this girl, who in her turn has given birth to your grandson Iacchus. Neither you nor I started this, nor are we the source of the conflict." I think Iambe/Baubo was saying more universally: "We are the life-givers, never forget that! We cannot become the destroyers, for our role is that of the recyclers." In her bawdy joke, was she not saying: "Lighten up! We must somehow manage it so that, as creators, we can continue to keep everything spinning, everything in balance. You must not turn your back on the whole mess, for it is our vulvas, our wombs, that are the center. We are the transformers!" This is not mere exhibitionism.

To emphasize the comic connection that existed between Demeter and Iambe/Baubo, the authors of *Demeter and Persephone in Ancient Corinth* have chosen as cover illustration a terra-cotta figure of a pregnant old woman, found in the excavations at Corinth, which they identify as a "pregnant actor," probably from the comedies. It is an image of a female impersonator, a grotesquerie with a padded belly. Greek women were never permitted to participate in Attic theater; all roles, as in Elizabethan theater, were performed by men. Thus the irony of the choice of this cover image, presumably of a male Baubo in drag, reinforces for me the distortions that occur when female myths, legends, and artifacts are looked at with old androcentric prejudices.

What is needed, in the language of Adrienne Rich, is "re-vision—the act of looking back, of seeing with fresh eyes, of entering an old text from a new critical direction," which "is for women more than a chapter in cultural history: it is an act of survival."[14] Baubo, that "nasty old crone," needs to be re-visioned by the women and men of today. Her image and her gesture have for too long been misconstrued as merely "a weakness for exhibitionism."

This book presents valid images of Baubo that are not pornography, but rather tributes to her powers. I offer and examine them as images of reverence not distorted by misogyny. It is time to move Baubo out of her dark little corner, to brush the encrusted spider webs from her form and to set her in her own proper niche. It is time to ask those persisting questions about her lineage, her rituals, and her jokes. That quality of humor is key, for references to Baubo usually carry a special quality of laughter. It is a chuckling, wry sort of humor, compounded of irony, compassion, and shared experience between women. It is laughter that has taken into account what Clarissa Pinkola Estés has called "the exploits of women, both real and mythological, who had used sexuality, sensuality, in order to make a point, to lighten sadness, to cause laughter, and in that way to set something aright that had gone wrong."[15] It is Baubo's sacred belly laugh.

. . . until sage Iambe,

with much jesting and joking, caused the holy lady

to smile and to laugh and to have a gracious heart,

and afterwards as well she pleased her moods.

—*Homeric* Hymn to Demeter[1]

Sage Iambe and Raucous Baubo

The clearest and earliest written evidence for sage Iambe as a functioning mythic personality is contained in a few brief lines in a beautiful long poem called the *Hymn to Demeter* (a fuller synopsis and translation of which appears in appendix 1). My term "sage" derives from the Greek adjective *kedn' eiduia* that is used to describe her. This phrase is translated in many ways, including "careful," "trusty," "thoughtful," "diligent," "perceptive," "knowing her duties," or, as above, "sage." I will use several of these possibilities interchangeably. The *Hymn* was one of thirty-three anonymous poems gathered together in antiquity, eventually becoming known collectively as the Homeric Hymns—though they were not written by Homer at all. The collection dates from the seventh century BCE and contains many archaic legends. We do not have all the poems in their entirety and some are badly fragmented. Scholars believe, however, that the *Hymn to Demeter* is complete.

The poem begins with a clear statement of its subject:

> I sing of lovely-haired Demeter, the awesome Goddess
> and of her slender-ankled daughter, who was abducted by Hades,
> with the connivance of Zeus, the loud-thunderer who sees all. (1–4)

The *Hymn* describes the rape and abduction of Persephone by Hades, lord of the underworld, and her descent into his realm (see fig. 2.1). It tells of Demeter's fury and her sorrow, of her long and weary search for her daughter, of her arrival at Eleusis in the disguise of an old nurse. It is at this point in the *Hymn* that Iambe makes her first and only appearance, in the role of a servant in the Eleusinian household. Demeter, disconsolate, has entered the great hall of the ruler of Eleusis and stands in the doorway. Metaneira, queen of Eleusis, immediately offers the impressive stranger a seat on the splendid couch, but Demeter refuses and remains standing, head down, full of remorse. "Sage Iambe" steps forward, offering a simple stool for the goddess, being careful to cover it first with a soft fleece. Demeter accepts, but continues in the grip of her sorrow:

> For a long time, silently, she sat there with sorrowing heart,
> responding neither by word or gesture, never smiling
> and without tasting either meat or drink . . .
> until Iambe, knowing her duties,
> with much jesting and joking caused the holy lady
> to smile and to laugh and to have a gracious heart. (198–205)

Alas, this splendid poem offers no further clues to Iambe's jokes or riddles or jesting verses. Her remarks must have been funny because Demeter raised her head, looked at Iambe, smiled, and laughed. The text makes it clear that careful Iambe pleased the deity's moods in "aftertimes" and that she continued useful to Demeter in other ways, remaining with her as servant or perhaps as one of her priestesses.

FIGURE 2.1 *Persephone vanishing into Hades. Detail from a Minoan cup. Phaistos, Crete. Ca. 2000* BCE.
(Lincoln, 1981, p. 75, fig. 25. Also see Kerenyi, 1967, p. xix.)

Because of the suggestive nature of Iambe's remarks to the goddess, implying coarse or lewd humor, and because other sources from Orphic literature and later commentaries describe Iambe as lame and halting in her gait, scholars once thought that the comical character Iambe was the original source of inspiration for the iambic meter of Attic Greek poetry, used for satiric invective in halting verses. But as Paul Friedrich points out, "The more relevant possibility is that iambic verse figured importantly in the Eleusinian Mysteries. Otherwise, Iambe's jesting and quipping may constitute a mythic precedent or charter for the obscene badinage among women, . . . or individuals of both sexes, that characterized . . . the Eleusinian Mysteries; such verbal behaviour, common in fertility rites in general, is thought to stimulate the productive powers of the Earth."[2] This link between Iambe's joking with Demeter and the fecundity of earth lies at the heart of much that developed at Eleusis and that will be explored in the course of this book.

The *Hymn* continues by telling of Demeter's stay at Eleusis, where, maintaining her disguise, she served as wet nurse for the new baby prince of Eleusis. It speaks of her never-ending grief and anger over the loss of her own child, Persephone, and of her terrible vengeance on both men and gods when she caused a cruel famine on earth. It recounts how Zeus was forced to act, finally allowing the return of Persephone from the underworld, and how mother and daughter were thus reunited.

The concluding sections of the *Hymn* tell of Demeter's reconciliation with the community of Olympian gods; how Demeter, with Persephone once again seated beside her, relented and allowed the earth to green. The close of the poem is concerned with the sacred rites and rituals that Demeter taught the people of Eleusis. The verses establish the legendary origins of the ceremonies in the worship of Demeter at Eleusis, mysteries that were repeated annually for hundreds and hundreds of years.

This poem has been interpreted by some in terms of "another ancient theme: that of consolation,"[3] with sage Iambe attending the grieving goddess with her jokes and gestures offered purely as acts of consoling diversion. I see the basic theme not as consolation but rather as the jubilant confirmation of woman's power and energy, expressed by Iambe in her nurturing concern and her earthy humor. For Iambe, jokes and jests are laughter *with* and are never used as laughter *against*. Her act not only consoles; it reenergizes Demeter, reestablishing her identity and role.

Bella Debrida makes that point in comments on the *Hymn* in a modern evaluation of feminist spirituality:

Despite the consolidation of patriarchal control, the hymn unequivocally acknowledges woman's power. Demeter, in response to a violent, anti-social act, refuses to extend Her procreative power to Earth as long as the violence of rape is permitted to go unpunished by the current race of man or gods. . . . Her action demonstrates that the power of life may be withheld as well as bestowed; that is, woman embraces all of life: birth and death, creation and decay. Irreverence or abusive treatment of woman, of Earth, and of their life-giving qualities brings about inevitable destruction.[4]

The transformation of sage and thoughtful Iambe, knowing her duties, into the raucous Baubo, with her ceremonial gesture of *ana-suromai*, took place in later centuries. Further written evidence for Baubo can be found in Orphic poems. Orphism, an aspect of Greek religion that began around the seventh century BCE, was gradually intermingled with Dionysian worship and became widespread in all layers of Greek society. The origin of Orphic writings, doctrines, and rituals was attributed to the archaic mythic poet Orpheus, who was reputed to have cast spells on animals and trees.

The persona of Baubo appears in variant forms in different fragments of Orphic writings, but most have clear similarities to the basic pattern of the Homeric *Hymn to Demeter*. In some Orphic versions, Persephone's rape took place in, or close to, Eleusis; and Demeter in her wandering search was received and welcomed into the humble cottage of a poor couple named Dysaules ("ill-housed") and his wife, Baubo. They attempted to comfort the goddess to the best of their abilities. Their sons, Triptolemos and Eubuleus, were herdsmen who had witnessed the rape while out in the fields with their flocks. In another Orphic fragment, one son of Dysaules serves as guide for Demeter and conducts the sorely distressed goddess mother down into the realm of Hades, there helping her search for her daughter. The other brother, the swineherd Eubuleus, was said to have provided the pigs on which Persephone and her underworld ravisher had first traveled down to Hades' realm.[5]

Charles Picard, a French scholar who has made an important study of Baubo's Orphic sources, reports that Dysaules and Baubo are mentioned in some texts as representatives of the ruling family of Eleusis and that they had two sons and two daughters as well. In Picard's view this overt association between actual families and Orphic characters may have been an attempt among the leading Athenian families around Eleusis to establish genealogical claims of glory as the original hosts to the goddess. He speculates that such lineages were invented and fought for in rivalries over sacerdotal or priestly privileges.[6] Thus King Dysaules and his wife, Baubo, in the Orphic poems, were contending with King Keleos and his wife, Metaneira, in the pseudo-Homeric version for the honor of entertaining and establishing Demeter at Eleusis.

An Athenian author named Philochorus, who lived during the middle of the fourth century BCE, wrote prolifically about ancient myths and religion. In his myth, Iambe is the daughter of the great god Pan and the goddess Echo. This Iambe also stood before the grieving Demeter and attempted to console her with absurd stories, jokes, and gesticulations. Philochorus reports that there was a sanctuary to Echo on the Holy Way leading from Athens to Eleusis, offering the possibility that her daughter, Iambe, also had a place in the Eleusinian Mysteries.[7]

A very different Orphic myth about Baubo had its origin in Phrygia, across the Hellespont in Asia Minor. The Phrygian Baubo was said to have a daughter called Mise ("me say"). They were closely associated "nocturnal creatures, of an oblong shape, shadowy, like those terrestrial powers that abhor the light and have an affinity for cavities (*koilia*), and whisper to humans sinister murmurings born from indistinct words."[8] It is in this role of night creatures or bogies that Baubo and her daughter Mise were frequently associated with Hecate, the great mistress of transformations. Hecate and the Phrygian Baubo both had connections to the transformative powers of a female toad or frog who had magical powers.[9] This recurrent Baubo/Hecate/toad connection will be examined in chapter 7. The metamorphic activity of Baubo and the toad was a popular ancient idea. Baubo and the toad were both feared and loved magical creatures able to perform many services.

The rude and jesting manner of Iambe/Baubo reappears in many countries and not only in archaic times. In many parts of the world, funeral directors employ professional jesters to relieve the mourners. In Sardinia, "this custom used to be explained by a story about the Virgin Mary similar to the Demeter myth. When she [Mary] was mourning the death of her Son, the animals tried unsuccessfully to comfort her, until a frog made her smile by boasting that her own grief was much worse, since she had lost seven children run over by a cartwheel."[10]

Other similar frog stories come from Rome, Romania, and contempo-

FIGURE 2.2 *Iambe offering the* kykeon *to Demeter.*
(An original woodcut print by W. M. L.)

rary Greece, where an analogous tradition exists as part of the modern festival of St. Domnēs, during which the local midwife is "adorned with gilded flowers, onion and garlic tresses, necklaces of dried figs, currants and carob beans, and one large onion. . . ." As she sits upon a makeshift throne, the women file by her and present her with gifts. The old women, who traditionally attend the midwife, offer her a phallic-shaped object "made from a large leek or sausage" to kiss. Then the garlanded midwife is escorted through the streets of the village by the women "as if she were a bride." Singing and dancing characterize the entire event, and "their songs and jokes are extremely lewd. Needless to say, all the menfolk stay indoors on St. Domnēs Day."[11]

Whether as queen of Eleusis, a rustic farmer's wife, the daughter of Echo, or a frog or toad, Iambe/Baubo is a figure celebrated in the Orphic legends for the feat of having made the grieving goddess smile (see fig. 2.2). By offering Demeter the reviving ritual cup of *kykeon* (a potion of meal, mint, and water), she not only gave solace and thus shared in the sorrows of the Great Mother but also reenergized the goddess to be nurturer of earth's fecundity. The continuation into modern times of some of these so-called "obscenities" at both death and birthing ceremonies does not mean that ancient customs have been preserved intact in an unbroken pattern. The jokes and jests of Iambe/Baubo are dim echoes of an idea. The laughter she stirs and the skirt-lifting gesture of *ana-suromai* are surprisingly potent ritual signals of the obligation to honor the needs of the earth. They are reminders that humans still hold responsibility for waking "the rich udder, the life-giving earth." Like Demeter, human beings have the power to "encourage again the growth of the fruit that gives life to men."[12] Baubo's magical connection to this fundamental myth of power, nurturing, and fecundity is the source of her lingering metamorphic echo through the millennia to our own time.

CHAPTER THREE

This is the procession

of old leathery mothers,

the moon's last quarter

before the blank night,

mothers like worn gloves

wrinkled to the shapes of their lives,

passing the word from hand to hand,

mother to daughter,

a long thread of red blood, not yet broken.

—*Margaret Atwood*[1]

Baubo Verified

Because I am dealing with Baubo as a presence that both pre-
cedes and succeeds Greek culture and because her name is so rarely mentioned in Greek records, the actual existence of Baubo as a recorded mythic
personality may begin to appear fanciful. In the absence of any identifying
label of Iambe/Baubo on vase fragment, seal, coin, or statuette, it is reas-
suring to find the name "Baubo" in three Aegean stone inscriptions. The
"long red thread" of Margaret Atwood's poem does surface; the presence is
a palpable reality.

Charles Picard and Maurice Olender both cite sources for two temple inscriptions that include the name "Baubo." On the earlier example, a dedicatory stone from the fourth century BCE, found on the Aegean island of Naxos, "Baubo" is listed after the names of Demeter, Zeus, and Kore.[2] The second inscription, from the first century BCE, was found on the neighboring island of Paros, which was for centuries an important center of worship of the ancient grain goddess. This marble plaque from Paros was dedicated by an unidentified woman to Demeter Thesmophoria (giver of law and civilization), and again Baubo's name is inscribed after those of Hera, Demeter Thesmophoria, Kore, and Zeus.[3]

Yet a third inscription, from the first century CE, was found near Priene at Magnesia on the Mediterranean coast of Asia Minor. On this marble plaque Baubo takes her place among an honorable company of wet nurses. Her name is listed with two other women as a legitimate descendant of the illustrious Ino of Cadmus, who was reputed to have had the distinction of breast-feeding the infant Iacchus (the name given to Dionysus at the breast).[4]

Olender adds further etymological verification of Baubo as nurse in his study of a group of commonplace ancient Greek words that stem from the root *bau-*. He points out that "Baubo has the sense of the particular body movement of a nurse rocking an infant."[5] And he lists the following Greek words that incorporate the idea of a nurse's movements:

baubauein	to sleep, to lull to sleep
baubalidsein	to rock
bakale	a cradle
baubon	a pacifier, later used as a term for dildo[6]

Because the root syllable *bau-* had a strange and foreign sound for the ancient Greeks, it may well have been an alien importation, further suggestion that Baubo's origins lie outside Greece. On the basis of other etymological clues, far older traces emerge, which seem to point to Sumerian-Babylonian culture as a possible origin of Baubo. A number of variations on the name Ba occur in Mesopotamian and other early Middle Eastern civilizations. In Sumer, for instance, there was a primeval goddess called Bau who ruled over the dark waters of the deep or the void (see fig. 3.1). A fragment of a clay tablet dating from 2500 BCE has been recovered from the Sumerian city of

FIGURE 3.1 *The Sumerian goddess Bau. Fragment from a stone pillar. Lagash, Sumer. Ca. 2200 BCE. The Louvre, Paris.*
(*Encyclopédie photographique de l'art*, vol. 1, p. 226, fig. a; Parrott, 1961, p. 235, fig. 288)

Lagash; this tablet once listed over seven hundred priestesses, priests, and attendants who participated in the consecration of a temple belonging to the goddess Bau, clearly a divine person of importance.[7] Bau was worshipped in Phoenician religion well before 1000 BCE as a primordial goddess who personified the mother of divine races. She had many names. As Baev, she was the guardian of the source, the well, the cave, hole or entrance, and perhaps the womb and vulva. In one Phoenician myth she is the wife of a wind god.[8] The Syrian version was the goddess Baalat, whose husband, Ba'al, was a young storm god, or lord of mountains. He became the ruler-god of Ugarit, which was a thriving port city on the northern coast of Syria (ca. 1200 BCE). There, Baalat (alias Anat) was Ba'al's consort and his sister. As Baalat, or Anat, she was a powerful goddess of both love and war.[9]

Bau—alias Baau, Baev, or Baalat—threads her way from Sumer passing through Ugarit and Phoenicia, moving perhaps via Rhodes and Cyprus on to Crete. It is also possible that "the long thread of red blood, not broken" then led from Egypt to the Greek mainland. It is possible that this eastern Bau at some point combined with a Thracian Baubo, who was reputed to be an ancient queen of the underworld. There seems to be no single traceable route for Baubo, but regardless of the tangle of her paths, the central concept of Bau, Baalat, or Baubo—wherever and whenever she appeared—is connected with hole, entrance, cave, womb, or vulva, and her role is usually that of a fecund nurturer or nurse (see fig. 3.2).

The early twentieth-century Egyptologist Margaret Murray strongly favored the theory of an Egyptian origin for Baubo:

> The legend of Baubo is known only through the Greek accounts. . . . As the Greek form of the goddess's name is written indifferently as Baubo or Babo it is probably derived from the goddess Bebt, the female counterpart of the god Beb. Of these two deities little is known. . . . The cult of Beb and Bebt is best known in the First Intermediate Period, particularly in the VIIth Dynasty [2250–2050 BCE], when personal names compounded with Beb are very frequent. Figures of Beb and Bebt are unknown in pharaonic times, or at least have not been recognized; and it seems significant that under the Ptolemies and the Romans, when the deities of the common people became important, the Baubo figures should occur in great numbers.[10]

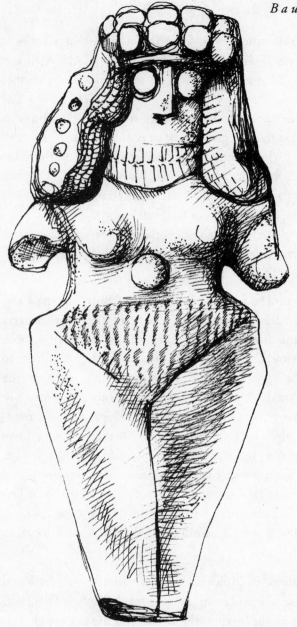

FIGURE 3.2 *A Sumerian goddess of fertility and fecundity. Terra-cotta from Tello, Sumer. Ca. 2900 BCE. The goddess is shown wearing the necklace of the divinity. The holes on the right side of her elaborate coiffure may have been used for decorations of fresh flowers, ribbons, or small rings. The Louvre, Paris.*
(*Encyclopédie photographique de l'art*, vol. I, p. 211, fig. c.)

The work of Murray and others encourage the notion that Baubo or Baubo-like figures and personalities were widely known in the Mediterranean world. (I discuss Murray's references to the Hellenistic figurines found in Egypt and Italy in chapter 9.)

Yet another curious link, which Murray does not mention, connects Baubo to Egypt—the Egyptian cat goddess Bast. Bast was one of the most popular Egyptian deities, whose main temple was at Bubastis on the Nile. She was a gentle goddess venerated by women. Not only does her name include the *ba*-root, but Baubo's *ana-suromai* (the skirt-raising gesture) was a well-documented aspect of the rituals at Bast celebrations.

Herodotus gives a vivid account of the Egyptian version of *ana-suromai* in his *Histories*, written in the last half of the fifth century BCE (see fig. 3.3). According to his presumably eyewitness report:

> Now, when they sail on the river to the festival of Bubastis, men and women together crowd into each barge. Some of the women carry castanets and make much noise, while other women play flutes; both men and women sing and clap their hands. Whenever they pass close to a town, they bring the barge in nearer to the river bank, and then the women do various things that I have described. They also shout out abuse and yell mocking jests and jokes at the village women standing along the river's edge. Some of the women on the barges perform dances, and then, standing up, they hitch up their skirts. On arrival at Bubastis they make a festival with many sacrifices, and more wine is said to be drunk at this feast than during all the rest of the year. According to the reports of the inhabitants of Bubastis, as many as seven hundred thousand men and women (including children) assemble together here.[11]

With its flutes and castanets, its buffoonery and ribaldry, its sacrifices and wine, its jokes bandied between pilgrims, and the frank display of genitalia exhibited by the women on the boats to the women on the river bank, this great and raucous celebration on the Nile typifies the kind of women's rituals performed at a number of sites in the ancient world.

Four hundred years later, another such traveler, Diodorus Siculus, reported the persistence of similar rituals at another Egyptian site, in Memphis. Around the middle of the first century BCE, he recorded that women

FIGURE 3.3 *An Egyptian musical celebration similar to the festival at Bubastis. Detail of a tomb painting from Thebes. Ca. 1400* BCE. *British Museum, London.*
(Woldering, 1963, pl. 145, fig. 47.)

enacted identical ritual gestures of *ana-suromai*. He noted that in the vast temple of the Serapeum at Memphis, women presented themselves by lifting their gowns before a sacred bull called Apis, whom they worshipped as a manifestation of the all-powerful god Ptah[12] (see chap. 9). These reports by Herodotus and Diodorus Siculus, four hundred years apart, are important pieces of evidence that fit into the bigger Baubo puzzle. They confirm that Baubo's *ana-suromai* and her laughter continued to play a vital part in agrarian fertility worship in many areas of the Mediterranean.

It is possible, as Murray and other scholars believe, that the festivals of Eleusis and Thesmophoria honoring Demeter and Kore retained parts of these same ritual themes from Egypt, and that Baubo unveiling her bare belly before Demeter actually repeated the gestures of the Egyptian priestesses before Bast at Bubastis and the women before the bull Apis at the temple of Memphis. It is also possible, however, that the presence of

Iambe/Baubo at the Attic festivals came not via Egypt, but from much earlier pre-Greek gynocentric societies in which women's basic connection to the fecundity of the earth was better understood as essential and sacred.

If Iambe/Baubo was simply an archaic holdover, why was she tolerated by the later Greek hierarchy at sacred and solemn ceremonies? Were her jokes and impudent behavior regarded as convenient release mechanisms for societal tensions? Was her "obscene" gesture accepted as a safety valve defusing explosive sexual attitudes? Answers to these questions can be found by examining certain important festivals, specifically the Thesmophoria and Eleusis.

CHAPTER FOUR

Maidens and begetters of children, join in this song!

All praise to Demeter, nurse of man

and giver of ample measures of corn.

As the four white-maned horses convey the basket offerings,

the great Goddess—the ruler of wide dominions—will come to us,

bringing bright spring and summer, winter and autumn,

and will safeguard us for yet another year.

—Callimachus, "Hymn to Demeter"[1]

Festival Sacrament, Sacred Laughter

Women might well have chanted these and the following words at the annual festival of Thesmophoria; they were written for a woman's religious ceremony in Alexandria by the poet Callimachus, who lived between 310 and 240 BCE. Only a gentle stretch of the imagination is required to include the spirit of Iambe or Baubo in this procession.

As we traverse the town barefooted with our hair flowing loose,
so shall our feet and heads forever be free from harm.

As the offering bearers carry baskets heaped with gold,
so we shall acquire gold in endless profusion.
Let the uninitiated women follow only as far
as the Prytaneion [town hall], but let the initiated women
enter the sanctuary of the Goddess, all those younger than sixty.
But those heavy with age, or the ones who entreat the help
of Eileithyia [goddess of childbirth], or whoever is in pain—
they need go no further than their legs can carry them.
Demeter will provide all things in plenty
as they approach her temple.
  Praise the Goddess, preserve this city in harmony
and prosperity, and ensure a full harvest from the fields.
Nourish the cattle; bring fruits; bring ears of corn;
and bring in the harvest.
Nourish peace as well, so that he who sows may reap.
Be gracious to me, O thrice invoked, great Lady of the Goddesses.

The spirit of Baubo would not have been forgotten by the basket bearers who moved slowly on their way toward the temple. The women over sixty, resting on the steps among the younger pregnant women, would have recalled the *ana-suromai* and chatted together, relishing the old tales of Baubo's boisterous behavior and her jokes.

The roots of Greek religion push far back into prehistory, to a time when earth and nature goddesses were worshipped as the embodiment of humankind, animals, the land, and the sky. Through the techniques of radio carbon dating and dendrochronology, it is now generally accepted that probably sometime between 4300 and 2800 BCE, three successive waves of northern warlike nomadic tribes invaded from the steppes of southern Russia or from the Balkan region. They overcame the earlier gynocentric cultures, imposing their own patriarchal cults, rituals, and religious systems of aggressive sky gods. Eventually an uneasy synthesis between the archaic chthonic goddesses and the invading sky gods was achieved, but a precarious sexual balance always remained among the Olympian pantheon. Greek state religion gradually evolved, with its rich heritage of myth, literature, and ceremony. It evolved into a religion that "certainly bears the stamp of its prehistory, but of a prehistory which is an infinitely involved network of interrelations. . . . There is no single origin of Greek religion."[2]

Eleusis, a small town just northwest of Athens, was the most important site of annual religious celebration in Demeter worship. Thesmophoria was not a site but an autumn season of celebration observed all over Greece for Demeter Thesmophoros (bringer of treasures). Both became carefully controlled state religious festivals reflecting multiple archaic origins. The story of Demeter and her lost child is one of the central primeval myths, which in time was transformed into a sacred drama and accepted as a metaphor for plant and human cycles of birth, resurrection, and death (see fig. 4.1). Some traces of the earlier women-revering rituals remained in ceremonial sacrifices, sacraments, and rituals at the festivals, but other important elements of song and dance, garlands, masks, and costumes vanished. Some of these rituals, like Baubo's, were revised and sanitized over the centuries.

Excavations conducted at the site of Eleusis have uncovered traces, dated ca. 1450 BCE, of a simple shrine constructed over an underground chamber. Such underground chambers, called *megara*, were known as sacred areas used for·storing seeds and grain or for burials of the dead. Thus there is reason to believe that rituals may have been performed at this site for more than two thousand years. By the fifth century BCE, Eleusis had become an impressive complex of sacred buildings and handsomely decorated open spaces, and the ceremony to Demeter and Kore held there had developed into a festival that was at the center of pan-Hellenic religious life. The yearly festival at Eleusis lasted for eight days of well-orchestrated ceremonies. Thousands attended from all over the Mediterranean region.

There were two parts to the ceremonies at Eleusis. The first ceremonies were open to all and occurred in the public spaces, where initiated and uninitiated participated together in a series of processions, purification rites, and sacrificial rituals. Everyone was permitted to join in these first five days at Eleusis; everyone, that is, "who had pure hands and intelligible speech," two requirements intended to exclude murderers and barbarians. There was no gender discrimination. Women of all classes, slaves and foreigners, prostitutes and citizens' wives, could, and did, attend the first five public days. At the close of the fifth day, a procession of initiates and officials set out to walk the fourteen miles of the Sacred Way that led from

FIGURE 4.1 *Detail of a clay plaque dedicated to Demeter and Persephone, suggestive of a rite of the Eleusinian Mysteries. Found at Eleusis. Ca. 300* BCE. *Athens National Museum.*

(Harrison, 1980, p. 558, fig. 158; Mylonas, 1972, fig. 88.)

Athens to the temple of Demeter at Eleusis. Priests and priestesses carried ancient cult statues of the goddess and Kore, while celebrants held various holy objects enclosed in caskets. And, just as in Callimachus's hymn, there must have been music and chanting.

Late in the afternoon of the fifth day, at a certain spot where several small streams marked the boundary between Eleusis and Athens, a traditional bit of clowning took place. Masked and cloaked figures gathered there on a narrow bridge, and as the procession went by, the buffoons jeered at all those passing, making lewd gestures and shouting obscenities. They were an accepted part of the festivities. The Greeks had a word for this species of clowning: *gephyra* means bridge, and so *gephyrizo* came to mean to abuse from a bridge or to revile. It is not surprising, therefore, to find that scholars ever since Hesychius have attempted to find an Iambe/Baubo persona among the *gephyristai* on that bridge. It is a matter that cannot be proved, but surely she would not have been out of place in that throng.

Aristophanes, in his comedy *The Frogs*, uses just such a chorus of drunken Baubo-like figures, placing them on the Sacred Way bridge, where they sing and dance on their way to the night festival. The chorus chants:

> Sing now, and let the festival begin.
> Now we're well fortified,
> Let's get into our stride;
> To the sweet flow'ry meadow let's march off in pride;
> At distinguished bystanders
> We'll jest and we'll jeer;
> It's the feast of the Goddess, we've nothing to fear.[3]

Historical evidence shows that this kind of buffoonery was not unique to Aristophanes or to Eleusis and that other Greek agricultural festivals had similar irreverent and raucous incidents. On these occasions it was customary for designated people to chant ribald and mocking songs, even obscenities. Such chanting was recognized as a means of stimulating fertility.

At Eleusis, such ceremonies, processions, and clowning occurred only during the first five public days. Everything that took place the following three days of the festival was kept absolutely secret. On those days of the Mysteries, known as the *Teletai*, or completion, only individuals who had been purified and initiated at ceremonies held weeks earlier could attend. Those rites have never been described, and no details of the days of solemn ritual at Eleusis have ever been revealed. The words of the Homeric *Hymn to Demeter* state, "In no way are these matters to be violated or pried into, nor are they to be spoken, since great reverence for the gods must silence the voice."[4]

Even today, despite generations of scholarly research about Eleusis, the cult of the Mysteries remains open to speculation. We know vaguely of immersions in the river and sea, of sacrifices of pigs, of sacred cakes that were exchanged, displayed, and eaten, of sacred potions drunk, and of a holy drama performed by initiates mimicking the birth of a divine child. We hear rumors of Baubo being there, but the greater part of these ceremonies, or *Teletai*, remain unknown. The same secrecy applied to the graphic arts, and we have no images of the Mysteries. "Not every representation of Demeter and Persephone in vase painting or sculpture illustrates an aspect of the Mysteries. The artists, like the writers, found themselves bound by restrictions, and the artist who dared divulge secrets . . . would have run the danger of prosecution."[5]

In chapter 5, I will discuss some of the divergent opinions on the thorny question of Baubo's presence at the festivals. Scholarly passions run high on this subject. But aside from the buffoonery incident on the bridge, the only written confirmation for Baubo's presence comes from the biased commentaries written centuries later by theologians of the early Christian Church, who frankly expressed their opposition to these pagan rituals. It is through their shocked accounts that we learn of Baubo's "scandalous behavior."

Clement of Alexandria (150–215 CE), Eusebius, bishop of Ceasarea (260–340 CE), and Hesychius of Miletus (who died ca. 550 CE) presented different accounts of Baubo's actions. Clement reports: "And thus speaking, she [Baubo] hoisted up her robes and displayed all of her body in a most unseemly manner. The child Iacchus [Persephone's son] was there, and laughing he thrust his hands under her breasts. When the goddess observed this, she smiled in her heart. And then she graciously accepted the gleaming vessel in which the *kykeon* was held"[6] (see fig. 4.2).

This account, like those of other Christian observers, was written many centuries after the golden age of Athens when Eleusis flourished. By 389,

FIGURE 4.2 *The* ana-suromai *of Baubo as it might have been performed before Demeter.*

(Linoleum print of an original design by W. M. L.)

the Byzantine emperor Theodosius had issued an edict forbidding the worship of pagan deities, and in 395, the Eleusinian sanctuary was completely destroyed by the Goths. The Eleusinian Mysteries had ended. The Byzantine scholar and historian Michael Psellus (d. 1078) wrote about Eleusis. As already mentioned, Jane Harrison shows that he described the ancient rituals in terms of demonology. He included Baubo as a manifestation of such a demon. Perhaps Psellus was reflecting the ancient, acknowledged kinship of Baubo to Medusa and her Gorgon sisters. As the sacred and profane aspects of feminine nature became divided, as her feared, dark side became dominant and the sacred elements were split off, Baubo as

Gorgon became one of the many prototypes of the female sexual demon, a destroyer as well as a protector (see chap. 8).

Thesmophoria, in contrast to the massive solemnities of Eleusis, was a smaller, more intimate women's affair, but Baubo's presence was still felt. The three-day festival occurred each October at the time of autumn grain sowing, with traditional and sacred rituals performed solely by women. Men were absolutely excluded. The origin of the Thesmophoria is obscure, and many of its ceremonies involving seeds and suckling pigs may have been of extraordinary antiquity.

Herodotus had observed mystery rituals in Egypt that he cautiously suggested had similarities to a rite performed at the Thesmophoria. According to Herodotus, the daughters of Danaus brought this particular ritual from Egypt and then taught it to the Greek women.[7] Whatever the origins, the Grain Goddess remained the focus of worship at Thesmophoria, giving her name Demeter Thesmophoria, or the treasurer and lawgiver, to this agrarian festival. Agriculture was understood as the gift of Demeter, the gift of settled life, of marriage, and of the beginnings of civilized law. On these three holy days at the Thesmophoria women gathered together to mourn with the goddess and to console her for the loss of her daughter; the rituals were intended to comfort the goddess, following the pattern set by Iambe/Baubo in the *Hymn*. The rituals included seed magic, sacrifices of piglets, rites acknowledging the underworld power of the snake, and the return of Persephone to earth. But always—after the solemn rites and after the communal mourning—always there was laughter, when Baubo's gift of joke and jest was shared among women. The jesting, mocking songs, clowning gestures, and use of foul language (*aischrologia*) were, as Walter Burkert makes clear, integral to Thesmophoria:

As the women celebrate on their own at the expense of the men, the antagonism between sexes is played up and finds release in lampoonery. . . . [The] Greek evidence, however, always points most conspicuously to the absurdity and buffoonery of the whole affair: there is a conscious descent to the lower classes and the lower parts of the anatomy, mirrored in the talk of mythical maids. Just as pomp and ceremony contrast with everyday life, so does extreme lack of ceremony, absurdity, and obscenity; a redoubled tension arises between the two extremes, adding further dimensions to the festival.[8]

There is considerable speculation over whether Thesmophoria was a women's puberty initiation or whether it was, as Karl Kerenyi says, "nothing else but the periods of the Greek women elevated to an annual festival, accommodated with this name in the sphere of Demeter Thesmophoros."[9] For "so long as the women had their periods, experience proved that they possessed fertility. It was in the spirit of the Demeter religion . . . that they were able, during these days especially, to do something for the fertility of the earth, because they were sure of their own fertility."[10]

Burkert agrees with Kerenyi that "perhaps experiences and behavior connected with menstruation could have provided the model for the ritual structure of an annual festival in which women assure themselves of their own peculiar nature, denied to men. At the core of the festival there remains the dissolution of the family, the separation of the sexes, and the constitution of a society of women; once in the year at least, the women demonstrate their independence, their responsibility, and their importance for the fertility of the community and the land."[11]

Betty De Shong Meador, basing her work on that of Kerenyi, Harrison, and Burkert, has recreated a scene from Thesmophoria. Here is her description of the Nesteia, the second day of the festival, a solemn day of fasting:

> The remainder of the day the women fast seated on the ground. They say the women imitate the ancient way of life. They move into the primitive way their grandmothers knew. They sit upon the ground. They sit in ritual silence in the sacred fields. . . . The women are one with the earth. The life of the earth and the life of the women comingle, an open exchange, a bond of kin. . . . The fast is broken at sunset. In a ritual gathering the women eat sacred cakes. The cakes are replicas of the great pudenda which sits on the altar. The silence is broken.[12]

The one food the women were allowed to eat during the second day of the fast was the pomegranate. The pomegranate with its astonishing number of seeds and brilliant red juice has long been seen as a complex symbol, combining womb or fertility with images of bloody death.

> Furthermore, the red color evokes associations not only of mortal wounds but also of menstrual blood, the blood of defloration, and the blood of parturition: blood of life as well as of death, sexual blood, woman's blood. . . . Death, life, male, female, and, above all, the irrepressible power of reproduction—are all found in the image of the pomegranate seed. It is this seed that Persephone takes within her body, literally incorporating it into her own being. With this seed, she becomes a new person: whole, mature, fertile, and infinitely more complex than before.[13]

The women's ritualized eating of pomegranate seeds may have been, therefore, a gesture symbolic of sisterhood with Persephone, who had been tricked into swallowing a pomegranate seed on her journey up from Hades' realm, and it may be that the succulent fruit was allowed to drip onto the earth instead of, or alongside of, the magic "moon blood." The pomegranate, symbol of uterine fertility, was also thought to bring about rebirth because of this underworld connection with Persephone. Eventually, Christian iconography absorbed this powerful symbol: Mary with the infant Jesus on one arm and holding a pomegranate in the other hand became popular in Catholic imagery.

During Thesmophoria, the women used both the pomegranate and another plant, lygos, in their blood-transformation rites. The species of lygos that grows in Greece is called agnuscastus, a flowering bush of the vervain genus, now called the "chaste tree," a name derived perhaps from archaic knowledge of the efficacy of its seeds, flowers, and leaves as an anti-aphrodisiac. It was also thought to repel snakes, and the women at the festival gathered heaps of lygos for their pallets inside their tents or shelters. But it was most noted as an herbal tea that stimulated menstruation. For nine days preceding Thesmophoria, the women initiates prepared and drank an infusion made from the crushed lygos leaves, and they continued to drink this potent tea throughout the three festival days.

Drinking lygos was believed to bring on menses, and thus it is conceivable that a kind of communal menstrual cycle was induced at the festival.

Communal menstruation is a well-documented phenomenon that can be achieved without the aid of herbal remedies. It has long been observed that, when groups of women live together in close quarters their periods often spontaneously become coordinated with each other and with the moon's cycle. This mysterious synchronicity remains unexplained, although doctors acknowledge it in the term "dormitory phenomenon."

The separate facets of the Mysteries of Thesmophoria—the rituals of moon blood, pomegranate seeds, infusions of lygos, piglet sacrifices, chanting priestesses, women's bawdy jokes—all are pieces of the pattern that shaped the festival. These rituals may be merely odd bits and pieces that have filtered down to us, surviving by the luck of history. They cannot be fitted together to form a seamless whole, because too many pieces are missing or twisted out of shape by cultural overlays. Yet the overall picture is still of a coherent set of symbolic rituals that must have been intended seriously to transform a woman's life. Surely, Baubo, who made the goddess laugh, was one of the transformers, one of the important missing pieces in this complex puzzle, and the absence of her jokes and her laughter is our great loss.

I have often wondered how I might respond if I could read one of Baubo's quips—if it had been miraculously preserved after transcription and dutiful annotation by some erudite Alexandrian grammarian of the first century. Would I smirk, faintly smile, chuckle, or, perhaps, double over with impolite guffaws? Maybe I would miss it entirely. Humor has an ephemeral quality, and archaic jokes can become soggy after the passage of twenty centuries. The great wit of Aristophanes, which reputedly delighted Athenian audiences (all men), has lost much of its savor through time and translation. Therefore, instead of yearning for Baubo's lost jokes, it is probably more productive to notice Demeter's reaction, her laughter.

We turn to that moment in the Homeric *Hymn* when Iambe/Baubo comes before that angry and deeply depressed goddess. The faithful old nurse provokes the awful Demeter to step aside from her rage and sorrow, reconsider herself, and break out in laughter. The joke that triggered the laugh is gone, but the bright laughter of the goddess has been remembered, recorded, and treasured. W. I. Thompson sums up the restorative function of such comedy:

This is the comic moment: man steps out of his tragic action, observes his self and his former universe, and laughs. . . . Laughter then involves detachment, and detachment is a fundamental form of freedom. This freedom is the central value in comedy . . . comedy offers a way out, a rebirth.[14]

The figure of Baubo with her impudent gesture offers "the way out," makes possible the moment of rebirth for Demeter; for by substituting laughter for anger, freedom becomes a possibility.

Thus Baubo has survived, stolen through as a faint memory from archaic women's rituals, to survive even the dominant Olympian religion. She survived as a comic link, understood primarily by women who valued her laughter and her ability "to steal through." They remembered her and understood her ability to reveal the sexual and emotional power of woman. They also understood her use of obscene humor (*aischrologia*) when confronting Demeter. She represented the mystic link between earth's fertility and human fecundity. The paradox is that in the Attic world—where men so carefully controlled and denigrated female sexual power—any trace of Baubo remained.

The story of Pandora illustrates how such antipathy reshaped myth. Pandora was originally an archaic Greek earth-goddess, her name meaning "giver-of-all-things" or "the all-gifted." In the eighth century BCE, when Hesiod came to compile his important patriarchal theological poem, *Works and Days*, he reset Pandora, not as a goddess, but as the first mortal woman. No longer giver of all things, she became the "bringer of all evils." In Hesiod's misogynist revision, Olympian Zeus orders the artisan god Hephaistus to create Pandora out of earth and water. The gods and goddesses are then summoned to clothe and adorn her, and Zeus commands the four winds to breathe life into her inanimate shape. Thus Pandora was created as a mortal being, singularly beautiful in face and body, but Zeus had contrived so that she was deceitful in nature and had a shameless mind. In Hesiod's version of the myth, this first woman set on earth was "an evil thing in which men might be glad of heart while they embraced their own destruction."[15] The remainder of Hesiod's myth is the part most widely known. Before sending Pandora to earth, Zeus gives her a great sealed jar, with solemn instructions never to open it. Zeus had filled the jar with his most malign curses against mankind: old age, sickness, insanity, vice, and passion. Pandora, forgetful of Zeus's instructions and moved by curiosity, pries open the jar, releasing upon mankind all the evil forces. Only hope was left, overlooked, tucked away under the lid of the jar.

By the fifth century BCE in Athens, female power was viewed as a blight and was feared as a dreaded anathema. Myths like Pandora and tales of Amazonian power were dimly remembered and regarded as scourges from the past that needed to be overcome and conquered. Baubo was another such myth. Eva Keuls has coined the apt term *phallocracy* for the reign of fifth-century Athens, a society "dominated by men who sequester their wives and daughters, denigrate the female role in reproduction, erect monuments to the male genitalia, have sex with the sons of their peers, sponsor public whorehouses, create a mythology of rape, and engage in rampant sabre-rattling, [and so] it is not inappropriate to refer to a reign of the phallus. Classical Athens was such a society."[16]

We now know from the work of archaeologists and historians that wives and daughters of Athenian citizens during the classical period lived extremely limited lives secluded within the women's quarters of the house, the *gynaeceum.* Athenian women (or, rather, "respectable" Athenian women) rarely left their homes except when escorted by servants or slave attendants. They never appeared at the public *agora,* or marketplace; they never attended the law courts or public banquets; and some scholars question whether women were permitted to be present at the great theater festivals.[17]

Customs did vary, however, from place to place. In Sparta women's lives were vastly different from those of their Athenian sisters, and Greek women in the cities of the Ionian coast and the islands led freer lives. Everywhere in the countryside peasant woman had more open, if not necessarily easier existences; and slavery of both women and men was an accepted component of the structure of Hellenic society. The majority of outdoor and indoor household tasks were performed by female slaves. The very large, well-organized, and profitable state-owned system of brothels filled with slave women flourished through the centuries, particularly in Athens and Corinth.

Religion was the single area where women were permitted to participate in the public life of the community, yet it must always be remembered that, especially in Athens, all cults were subordinate to and an integral part of the state, which was firmly in the hands of men. Thus a question remains: why in a society of such intense sexual segregation and antagonisms were women permitted to participate at Eleusis, and why were they encouraged to leave their secluded homes for the festival of Thesmophoria? Why were these sequestered women allowed the amazing freedom of camping out together in the open, in huts made of greenery where they played at independence for three eventful days? Why was a women's festival considered by the phallocracy to be of such vital importance that law courts and the council were closed for those three days; that prisoners were released; and that a law was passed obligating a citizen to send his wife to this female religious festival and stipulating that he pay the cost of her participation to the state coffers?

Other Greek religious festivals in which only women were permitted to participate included the ancient religious and athletic festival held in honor of Hera every fourth year at Olympia. For this occasion, sixteen chosen women wove a resplendent robe for the goddess; but the main events were athletic contests and a famous foot race with "virgins, who ran in order of age, the youngest first, and the eldest last."[18] The winning virgin was then crowned with an olive wreath and was identified with the moon. She was granted a share of a horned cow that had been especially sacrificed to the goddess Hera.

Because sexual antagonism seems to lie at the core of Attic society, it is not surprising to find it also embedded in Attic religious rituals. Keuls writes, "One would expect that in the city-state of Athens, where the polarization of the sexes was pronounced and rigidly enforced, ritual would reflect this split."[19] In Kreuls's view, the license of the festivals was a safety valve:

> The Greeks knew that one of the functions of ritual celebration is to release frustrations and pent-up energies and so help people get through life from one day to the next. . . . Since women bore the brunt of repression, one would anticipate more relief mechanisms for them than for men and this, too, seems to be the case. . . . Such rituals provide the intoxication of temporally limited freedom from social restraint, so that the participants will be the more pliable the remainder of the time.[20]

The use of religious cult or ritual as safety valve is of course familiar to us and continues into our times:

The politically oppressed often turn to ecstasy as a temporary means of possessing the power they otherwise lack: orgiastic ritual, secret cults, trances, and magic provided such outlets, especially for women, who could not justify meeting together for any other purpose.[21]

Orgiastic, ecstatic, and magic happenings very probably took place both at Eleusis and at Thesmophoria, but the "safety valve" theory does not completely explain why women were permitted to participate. For Ruth Padel the answer lies more in women's unique ability to create and nurture life.

However male society may confine women . . . it does crudely depend on their function of bringing things to light, of letting something emerge from themselves. Assigning women the ritual revelation of hidden sacred things, organizing a festival in which women themselves "come out," and elaborating in myth and poetry narratives in which women do escape . . . is a way of expressing, I suggest, and also of containing, women's closer connection with animal nature, through their capacity for childbirth. . . . Male society controls, monitors, and also, one might say, exploits, the animal nature in women (as men perceive them), which requires emergence, but which is perceived as destructive to society if not controlled by it.[22]

By the time of the Attic festivals, the story of Baubo was only dimly remembered. Yet Baubo's role was to reemphasize women's importance for the fecundity of earth and its peoples. The women's festivals—Baubo included—were reluctantly accepted because, despite male fears of "moon blood" and of women's collective power, men were faced with their own overriding need, with their concern to maintain the genetic purity of their lineage.

CHAPTER FIVE

When we have moved beyond the desolation of all our male vanities, from

the stock market to the stock pile of rockets, we will be more open and

receptive. Open and bleeding like that archaic wound, the vulva, we will be

prepared to receive the conception of a new civilization. Perhaps if we are

blessed by the old gods in the next civilization that will follow after this one

has played itself out, we will come to appreciate "the ancient and forgotten

wisdom."

—*William Irwin Thompson*[1]

Baubo and the Scholars

In the process of assembling these Baubo myths and images, I
have found that other scholars who have been there before me rarely
agreed among themselves, whether about Baubo's origins, the meaning of
her gesture, or her mythic significance.

Much "ancient and forgotten wisdom" is being reevaluated; many
things that seemed obscure or obscene only a few years ago now strike us
quite differently in the light of new archaeological discoveries and recent
feminist historical literature. Today it is possible to look at Iambe/Baubo,

at her Paleolithic and Neolithic antecedents, at the Hellenistic Baubo/Isis images, at the medieval Sheilah-Na-Gigs without the obscurantism and fog of past sexual attitudes.

Here is a sampling of differing historiographical viewpoints about Iambe/Baubo:

- Baubo is an interesting figure. She has all the characteristics of a creature of primitive popular imagination, a kind of bogey, and in later times became quite naturally an associate of the dread Hecate.
  —William K. C. Guthrie[2]

- But, we will soon find the best reasons—primarily historical and epigraphic—to show without doubt that Iambe/Baubo did exist, *almost all the time*, not only at the periphery of the Eleusinian cult, but one could say, at the precise center of the official mysteries.
  —Charles Picard[3]

- There are ugly sayings, *aischrologia*, and obscene exposures in women's festivals, especially at the Thesmophoria. . . . A name for mocking songs on such occasions is Iambos. . . . Iambe was made into a mythical figure, a maid who was able to cheer up Demeter after her sorrow and fasting.
  —Walter Burkert[4]

- Baubo was initially a personification current in Asia Minor of female fecundity.
  —Manfred Lurker[5]

- When Isis was mourning for Osiris, Baubo assumed the attitude represented in the figures, and thereby made Isis laugh and cease from lamenting. The legend is clearly late, for Baubo is called indifferently the hostess of Isis, the nurse of Isis, and is even one aspect of Isis herself.
  —Margaret A. Murray[6]

- Baubo, who is related to Aphrodite, belonged more to women than to men. She danced and sang before Demeter, told obscene (filthy or piggy) stories, and gave birth to laughter—specifically "belly laughs."
  —Nor Hall[7]

- One should have more respect for the bashfulness with which nature has hidden behind riddles and iridescent uncertainties. Perhaps truth is a woman who has reasons for not letting us see her reasons? Perhaps her name is—to speak Greek—*Baubo*?
  —Friedrich Nietzsche[8]

- One might point an accusing finger at the naturalists when they take as ribald a delight in Mother Nature as in the goddess Baubo herself—just because they have discovered a few little weaknesses in the good mother. Indeed, we recall having seen arabesques in which the sexual relations within a flower calyx were represented, in the manner of the ancients, in an extremely graphic way.
  —Johann Wolfgang von Goethe[9]

- It might be said that there is a certain aspect of consolation in Baubo's gesture which is intended to console Demeter for the loss of her daughter, by reminding her of her ability to have more children.
  —George Devereux[10]

- There is a powerful saying: *Dice entre las piernas*, "She speaks from between her legs." These little "between-the-legs" stories are found all over the world. One of them is the story of Baubo, a Goddess from ancient Greece, the so-called "Goddess of obscenity." She has older names, such as *Iambe*, and it appears the Greeks borrowed her from far older cultures. There have been archetypal wild Goddesses of sacred sexuality and Life/Death/Life fertility since the beginning of memory.
  —Clarissa Pinkola Estés[11]

In 1910 when Jane Ellen Harrison saw fit to leave untranslated her terse footnote on Baubo in her *Prolegomena to the Study of the Greek Religion*, very little had been written on the subject. Harrison, in company with Gilbert Murray, Robert Graves, George Frazer, and Rachel Levy, had just begun to turn her attention to what they all referred to as early matriarchal societies. They were tremendously stimulated by *Das Mutterrecht* of Johann Jacob Bachofen, published in 1861. If the subsequent discoveries on Crete and in the Balkans had been available to Harrison, no doubt she would have expanded her tentative vision of the role of women in prehistory and her contribution would have been considerably greater. Harrison writes:

> By a most unhappy chance our main evidence as to the Sacred Marriage of the mysteries [at Eleusis] comes to us from the Christian Fathers; their prejudiced imaginations see in its beautiful symbolism only the record of unbridled license. We may and must discredit their unclean interpretations, but we have no ground for doubting the substantial accuracy of their statements as to ritual procedure.[12]

I do not know whether Harrison would have agreed with Margaret A. Murray in the latter's formulation of Baubo as divine. I do not know if they ever met and had a chance to discuss these matters. Murray was an Englishwoman, a contemporary of Harrison, who, finally freed from the burden of family duties in her middle years, was able to study and start belatedly on her career. She trained and worked under the eminent Egyptologist Flinders Petrie. Perhaps her late start accounts for the fact that Murray is curiously free from the academic strictures of her time. Though she met with resistance and scorn from colleagues, she was able to work under Petrie and made many original and still controversial contributions. She was interested in the subject of witchcraft, viewing witches and their rituals as remnants of pagan religions. She was one of the earliest to make a connection between the Sheilah and pagan beliefs (see chap. 10), and she saw a distinct tie between these images and Baubo.

It was through her work as an Egyptologist that Murray became interested in Baubo, convinced that Baubo's origins were Egyptian, not Greek. In her 1934 article, "Female Fertility Figures," Murray asserted that the appeal of Baubo was "linked to the sexual side of woman's nature." She described Baubo's legend as "definitely connected with pleasure and laughter." In her opinion, "Baubo was as essentially divine as Isis or Ishtar, as Kybele or Aphrodite, but she was a goddess of women only. She belonged to that group of goddesses, such as the Bona Dea, from whose rites men were rigorously excluded. What those rites were can only be inferred from the vague hearsay evidence of male writers."[13]

In 1927, Charles Picard, a French classical scholar, published a detailed and provocative article summing up all the information about Baubo available at that date. Picard's study focused on Baubo's role at Eleusis, leaning heavily on Orphic sources and references from the early Christian Church Fathers. He arrived at the conclusion that Baubo was an integral part of the *hieros gamos*, the sacred marriage, thought by many to have been a part of the Eleusinian celebrations. The crux of Picard's argument is that Iambe/Baubo was a dual figure, with both a female and a male aspect, and that originally there had existed a couple, Iambe and Iambos, who then gradually evolved into the mythic Baubo and her consort Baubon. He agreed with earlier scholars who had speculated that Baubo and Baubon were personifications of far older anonymous sacred objects made of wood, clay, or bread dough that were regarded as symbols of the sacred pair and in the shape of vulva and phallus. Picard suggested that during the *Teletai*—the last, secret, most holy days of the Mysteries—celebrants ritually handled these symbolic objects in ceremonies exhalting the creation of life and ensuring the fecundity of the earth.

The principal foundation of Picard's argument is the writings of Clement of Alexandria, an early Christian theologian who wrote between 150 and 200 CE. Clement claimed that the secret sacred passwords used by initiates were "I fasted, I drank from the *kykeon*, I took out of the *kiste* [covered box], I worked and placed it back in the *kalathos* [basket] and from the *kalathos* into the *kiste*."[14] In Clement's pious view this had to be something obscene. In Picard's interpretation, the object taken out of the *kiste* was probably made in the shape of a vulva, and the second object exchanged from the *kalathos* was in the form of the phallus. The ritual manipulation of these objects by the celebrants, therefore, became a mimic form of the *hieros gamos*, which Picard called "un échange générateur," and which was intended to secure fecundity for the earth.[15]

Some fifty years later, another French scholar, Maurice Olender, turned his attention to the challenging question of Baubo. In an exhaustive 1985 article, "Aspects de Baubô," Olender reviewed all the material presented by ancient historians as well as the views of Picard, Harrison, Murray, and various German classicists. He writes: "The many modern ways of looking at 'l'affaire Baubô' has provoked a great deal of erudite polemics. . . . Scholars have generally chosen to confine their work to the question of the origins of Baubo. They ask: 'This brash one, did she or did she not play a role at Eleusis? . . . And if this was not the case, then the question close to the heart of the matter is to reveal the sources of the scabrous tale. Were they Orphic inventions, or were they foreign importations from Egypt or from the Far East?' "[16] Olender speculates as to whether Baubo's gesture can be taken at face value merely as an impudent bit of obscenity or whether it was a natural apotropaic expression or the averting of the Evil Eye common to many myths and rituals of fecundity:

> The holy nurse of the Homeric song would have derived from sexual symbols that came from the depths of archaic agrarian culture . . . from rites so old that, as early as the beginning of the sixth century, the raison d'être of these sexual symbols, partly anthropomorphized, was no longer understood. The symbols had been transformed into a couple, Iambe-Iambos, reticent refinements used as necessary euphemisms for other objects. . . . In other words, at Eleusis, Baubo and Baubon are the inherited remains of this very crude past.[17]

Olender thus sees a common motif that has existed in the rituals of many primitive agrarian religious celebrations, rituals where joyousness through dance and laughter became focused on natural sexuality, rituals subsequently described by scholarly analysts as obscene.

Whereas Picard and Olender place Baubo at the precise center of the Mysteries at Eleusis, George Mylonas maintains that the main evidence for Baubo is based on later Orphic, not traditional Eleusinian literature: "It can be stated categorically that the Eleusinian tradition has no place for Baubo at the site of Demeter."[18] Mylonas does not deny the existence of a Baubo, but he asserts that "the name was created after the fact, to personify the myth . . . that the creation of Baubo took place in a locality where the raising of clothes by women and the exhibition of their secret parts, accompanied by banter, obscene language and gestures, were related to the worship of some God or Goddess."[19] Mylonas then refers to the account of Bubastis by Herodotus and suggests that these ceremonies reflect a very old established practice, which could have given birth to Baubo and her story, and suggests further that the Orphic poets and, later, Clement absorbed these earlier stories from Egypt.

Mylonas marshals his facts with brilliant erudition. He is particularly critical of Picard's view that there was a specific ritual at Eleusis involving the handling, or, as he puts it, "the manipulation" of the *kteis* (vulva) and the phallus. Eleusis, in Mylonas's view, was a holy place, where sacred ceremonies of great purity took place, and therefore the manipulations as described by Clement are not tenable:

> The handling of the phallus and of the *kteis* is an unclean act, no matter how we may try to explain it. And yet chastity was a prerequisite for initiation [into the Mysteries]. Among the initiates we find not only women—young and old, married and single—but even children—boys and girls; and to expose these children to the act would have been criminal. . . . Since abstinence from intercourse and purification after it was required even for the average act of worship, how then can we admit even a symbolic act of the kind in the sacred Temple of Demeter?[20]

Mylonas reluctantly accepts evidence suggesting that the *hiera* (sexual marriage symbols) could have been displayed by a *hierophant*, a high priest or priestess, but he is absolutely convinced that the objects from the *kiste* were never given to the initiates to handle.

With a deft hand, Mylonas then plucks Baubo and her "unclean" rituals from the sacred festival of Eleusis near Athens. Instead, he argues that she perhaps was involved in later mystery cults held in an Egyptian Eleusis, a suburb of the Ptolemaic city of Alexandria. Mylonas suggests that these were later Hellenistic ceremonies that Clement and other Church writers had observed and that they were incorporated with various mystery cults of Rhea, Kybele, or Attis, rather than the earlier "purer" Attic festivals. Mylonas argues, "We may therefore conclude that we can learn very little, actually nothing of importance, as far as substance is concerned, about the Eleusinian Mysteries from Clement's statements; but we get from them the conviction that no acts, which even by Christian standards could be considered immoral, were included in these rites."[21]

This rerouting of Baubo to the world of Ptolemaic Egypt via a convenient suburban Alexandrian Eleusis is a neat evasion; it defuses and sanitizes any idea of female sexual power and defends the seat of Greek culture from the suspicion of "unclean" and "criminal" activity in the temple of Demeter. Mylonas thus can speak of a "depraved Baubo" conjured up by Orphic poets in contrast to a "trusted Iambe"[22] of the Homeric *Hymn*. Popular Isis/Baubo imagery from Egypto-Greco-Roman times may seem to support Mylonas's theory (see chap. 9); but it does not adequately explain the concrete proof of Baubo's name appearing alongside the gods on earlier inscriptions from Naxos and Paros. Nor can a theory of "borrowing" allow for the significance of Iambe/Baubo's role in the story of Demeter and her daughter.

The German classicist Walter Burkert describes Baubo at Eleusis as a dim memory of an earlier myth recounted in the Homeric *Hymn*, a legend that became distorted. Basically, Burkert is in agreement with Mylonas and does not accept that Baubo played an actual role at Eleusis. He too leaves open the possibility that she may have been present at later Demeter festivals that continued to take place on the islands of Paros or Naxos and in Messenia, Arcadia, and Sicily. Burkert offers another explanation for Baubo's involvement in the handling of symbolic sexual objects in the rituals of the *kiste* and *kalathos*. He suggests that the ritual objects exchanged were not necessarily meant to represent genitalia, but rather that they were simple tools used in the grinding of corn; that they were the mortar and pestle used to prepare the *kykeon*—the goddess's sacred drink of barley, honey, and pennyroyal described in the *Hymn to Demeter*. On the question of Baubo as hierophant or priestess, or of rumored orgies around the *hieros gamos*, Burkert firmly states, "We do not know the true course of events and have difficulty in coordinating the various allusions."[23] He sees a more logical place for Baubo in the segregated women's Attic festivals, such as the Thesmophoria, which he agreed may have included those disturbing elements of obscenity and blood.

> The women indulge in indecent speech, *aischrologia*; they may split into groups and abuse one another, but there must also have been occasions on which men and women derided one another. The *iambos* as a mocking poem has its origin here; Baubo, who makes the Goddess laugh by exposing herself, belongs to the Thesmophoria.[24]

Karl Kerenyi in his work on Eleusis does not overlook Iambe/Baubo. He recognizes the wise handmaiden Iambe's consolatory gestures to Demeter as told in the *Homeric Hymn*. Citing Clement, he recreates Baubo sitting with her legs wide apart in front of Demeter.[25] He then goes on to elaborate an explanation based on other, Orphic sources:

> The atmosphere of the festivals of Demeter allowed of coarse games and tales. According to this version, there was then no king in Eleusis but

only a poor peasant with his family. His name was Dysaules, "he in whose hut it was not good to live." His wife Baubo also had an eloquent name, it meant "belly." She did not hesitate to perform an obscene dance before the goddess and to throw herself on her back. In this way she made Demeter laugh.[26]

Kerenyi speculates, again using Orphic texts, that Demeter had descended into the underworld in her desperate search for her child and that there she encountered Baubo and her husband, Dysaules, "beings in whose house it was so ill to dwell."[27] In this colorful later mythic version, Demeter drives a serpent-drawn chariot as she searches for the ravisher of Persephone.

Kerenyi and C. G. Jung collaborated in 1949 on a volume of essays in which they explored many aspects of the Demeter-Kore myth. Jung saw Baubo as another form of the Earth Mother: "The figures corresponding to Demeter and Hecate are supra-ordinate, not to say over-life-size 'Mothers' ranging from the Pietà type to the Baubo type. The unconscious, which acts as a counterbalance to woman's conventional innocuousness, proves to be highly inventive in this latter respect."[28] And Jung goes on to say, "The often unaesthetic forms of the Earth Mother are in keeping with a prejudice of the modern feminine unconscious; this prejudice was lacking in antiquity."[29]

In an interesting work on women's rituals, Bruce Lincoln devotes a chapter to the "rape of Persephone." He writes, "The well-known myth of Demeter and Persephone is unquestionably the most important myth of classical antiquity to focus on the lives of women, and it is thus possible that it may have been tied to women's rites." Lincoln speculates that the *Hymn to Demeter* was possibly a "scenario of a young woman's initiation.[30] He goes on to suggest that

> at some point in prehistory, probably prior to the arrival of the Indo-Europeans in the Greek regions (ca. 1800 BCE?), a ritual resembling that described in the myth was actually performed for some or all women in these regions upon their arrival at puberty. Other members of the society, including men, participated in the ritual by taking the roles of other characters in the myth.[31]

Lincoln traces how these puberty initiations became Mystery initiations at Eleusis. He recognizes that "raucous Baubo—whose name literally means 'vagina'—was always represented as the personification of female genitals and that "such 'obscene' gestures are often found in connection with women's initiation and women's secret societies, enacted by women who are otherwise the soul of propriety."[32] His further contention is that

> when a young woman comes of age, or when women come together in the absence of men, the force of their sexuality is so great that it can no longer be suppressed. Although social norms may severely inhibit the direct expression of female sexual energy under ordinary circumstances, at these special moments it bursts forth in "obscene" gestures, songs, and stories, whereby women collectively celebrate the appearance of reproductive power in a new woman. Thus, when Demeter mourns the loss of her daughter, she simultaneously celebrates her transformation.[33]

George Devereux, in his book *Baubo, la vulve mythique*, considers Baubo as a strictly sexual symbol. Devereux, who styles himself as an ethnopsychiatrist, sees Baubo in terms of the "inventiveness of the unconsciousness" (in Jung's phrase), with Baubo acting as a stimulant rather than as "counter-balance to the conventional feminine innocuousness." In Devereux's opinion, Baubo's gesture of *ana-suromai* was intended to be a gesture of sexual arousal directed at Demeter, or "to turn Demeter on." His dubious contention assumes that a mourning woman is particularly susceptible to sexual arousal by another woman. He ranges deep into ethnographic literature to support his thesis and concludes that it is evident that Baubo's gesture, both by exposing her vulva and later by imitating the birth process, reminded Demeter that she might have other children to replace the lost Persephone. For Devereux, Baubo was able to help the goddess rediscover her normal state of sexual receptivity and thus give her pleasure.[34]

Devereux covers some of the same materials as Picard and Olender, but his point of view is far from theirs. He uses Baubo principally to support his own psychosexual theories and makes little effort to decipher the nuances of meaning that such an action must have had in its ritualistic setting in ancient times. He deals with important aspects of Baubo, but his glib treatment turns the material into a sort of case study for a Masters-and-Johnson-style Attic sexual report. In *Baubo, la vulve mythique* Devereux concentrates on the neurotic aspects of exhibitionism. He distinguishes between vulva display as used by women today, which he interprets as an insulting gesture used in quarrels between women, and the Baubo gesture as performed by a woman in front of a man, which he asserts has the meaning of witchcraft or "maléfice." He does, however, concur with classical historians that *ana-suromai* among women could once have been part of friendly and humorous, though perhaps bawdy, rituals that took place at secret female rites or at festivals.

It may seem that Baubo/Iambe has almost vanished beneath the weight of all this impressive erudition. She has been presented by (predominantly male) scholars as a night bogey frightening children or as a crude peasant nurse behaving inappropriately at festivals or as a masturbator intent on arousing Demeter. Clearly, Baubo is an affront to Jung's concept of "women's conventional innocuousness," for Baubo/Iambe was a creature of paradox. Where status was honored she sat beside the gods, but she also served them as servant or wet nurse. Where youth and beauty were exalted, Baubo/Iambe was seen as old and lame. Her frank behavior stimulated masculine sexual fantasies, and she substantiated male fears of the female as pollutant.

This ambiguity is reflected in the Greek language. *Hagnos*, a neuter noun, translates as a hallowed, holy, or sacred place or as an undefiled and chaste individual. *Hagneia* meant chastity. The verb *hagnidzo* was used specifically in the religious sense of "to clean or purify." But *hagos*, from the same root, had two meanings. It referred to any matter of religious awe or to a sacred being; in addition, *hagos* was also used for a curse or an abomination to refer to a polluted person or a defiled place.

Baubo with her double signals was *hagos* in both meanings of the word. She was sacred—and she was an abomination. Like the early goddess images she had many aspects. As woman, she contained in her body the complete round of life, death, and rebirth. Her "exhibitionism" before Demeter was a ritual reminder that through their bodies, they each contained the entire mystery of the creative cycle.

CHAPTER SIX

In the cave with a long-ago flare

a woman stands, her arm up. Red twig, black twig, brown twig.

A wall of leaping darkness over her.

The men are out hunting in the early light

But here in this flicker, one or two men, painting

and a woman among them.

Great living animals grow on the stone walls,

their pelts, their eyes, their sex, their hearts,

and the cave-painters touch them with life, red, brown, black,

a woman among them, painting.

—Muriel Rukeyser[1]

The Image Defined

At this point I ask the reader to make a great leap with me, moving from Iambe/Baubo, the servant of Demeter, to the caves and rock shelters of late Ice Age people. Baubo, as metaphor for the transformative power of female sacred sexual energy, was not a Greek invention. Long before the Sumerian goddess Bau, long before the female imagery of Bronze Age Cycladic or Egyptian culture, traces and glimmers of this same concept may be found. An examination of Paleolithic feminine iconography, therefore, provides illuminating connections. As Philip S. Rawson urges,

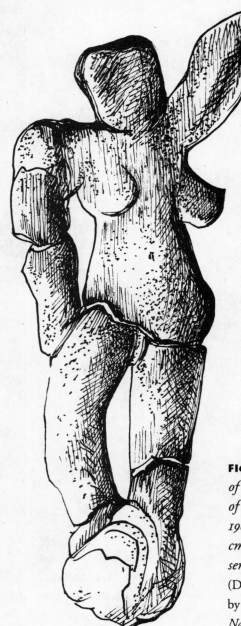

FIGURE 6.1 *The dancing "Venus" of Galgenberg—the most ancient of Paleolithic figurines. Found in 1988 at Galgenberg, Austria. 7.2 cm high and carved in green serpentine stone. Ca. 30,000* BCE. (Drawing by W. M. L. Cf. drawing by R. Bednarik from a photograph in *Nature* 342 [Nov. 23, 1989]: 345.)

"When we discuss all this material we must be prepared to take enormous leaps through space and time, even into our own epoch; for the persistence and distribution of basically similar imagery is truly staggering."[2]

Ice Age art is an unfamiliar phenomenon for most of us. This vast artistic heritage has only recently been unearthed and has not yet been assimilated into our historical pictorial vocabulary. Since 1864, there have been more than one hundred female figures found that span the period from 30,000 to 12,000 BCE. The first of the so-called Venus figurines was found in 1864 at Laugerie Basse in France. The cave of Altamira in Spain with its fabulous animal paintings was first discovered in 1879 and was promptly rejected as impossible and fraudulent. A generation passed before Abbé Breuil reexamined this cave in 1902 and declared it a genuine Paleolithic treasure. The caves at Lascaux were discovered in 1940. Every year new discoveries are made, each adding another facet to our understanding of human concepts of the sacred.

In 1988, a remarkable small sculpture named the Galgenberg Venus was discovered in excavations at the village of Galgenberg in Austria (see fig. 6.1). Its age is asserted to be 30,000 BCE, making it by far the oldest of the female figurines found to date. This sculpture measures 7.2 cm. in length (just under three inches) and is carved from a flat green serpentine stone. Its right hand and bent right leg are joined, with the right hand resting near the hip; the right arm is raised and shown folded back at the elbow. The left breast is carved in profile. The vulva is clearly indicated. This astonishing statuette has grace and movement, in contrast to later Ice Age figurines that are usually static and symmetrical forms with no perforations or protruding limbs. For most of us, images like the Galgenberg Venus and her later "sisters" are still unabsorbed, and their obesity and explicit sexual idiom can seem ugly and disturbing. But they are images that must be understood within their own context, not ours, and our eyes must adjust to their sacred implications.

We have acquiesced for a long time in the dictum that art, especially sacred art, was produced by the male of the species. As a result, we need this enormous leap through space and time and beyond our own prejudices if we are to look honestly at the images in the following pages—and to see them as art—as sacred art, as images that quite probably were created by women for other women, as well as for the men in their community. We

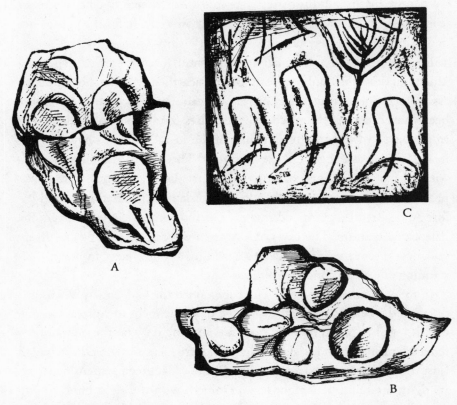

FIGURE 6.2 *Paleolithic images of the vulva. A and B show two limestone blocks with engraved designs. From a site in southwestern France (La Ferrassie and Cellier). Ca. 29,000 BCE. Musée des Antiquités Nationales, Saint-Germain-en-Laye. C is a detail of vulvas and plants from a cave painting at El Castillo, northwestern Spain. Ca. 14,000 BCE.*
(A and B: White, 1986, p. III, figs. 127, 128. C: Marshack, 1972, p. 319, fig. 187.)

are on the threshold of understanding that these earliest forms of art were not erotic images created for the arousal of either male or female sexual impulse but were made to serve spiritual needs. The ancient images of the vulva were not created as Paleolithic pornography. To their creators these objects were serious and sacred in purpose, a sophisticated iconography intended to stimulate the sacred forces of nature and keep them in balance.

It is in this tradition that Baubo the transformer has her place, proclaiming the regenerative power of the *koilia*, the womb.

The images presented in this chapter begin with the late Ice Age, dating from 30,000 BCE, and continue through the long epochs of the Neolithic, ending with the art of the Bronze Age, circa 1200 BCE. Until the discovery of the Galgenberg figurine, it was assumed that the vulva images carved in stone and found in caves and rock shelters at La Ferrassie and Abri Cellier in the Dordogne region of France, dated circa 30,000 BCE, were the most ancient known art (see fig. 6.2). Other stones with carved or painted vulva shapes have been found in various other Ice Age sites in Europe. They vary in size and shape; some are oval, others triangular; some stand by themselves engraved on stone fragments found deep inside caves; others were painted on rock shelters in conjunction with animal images. Some of these Paleolithic vulva symbols are strikingly realistic, whereas others are highly abstract, so that the part frequently stands for the whole.

We now know that the vulva as a symbol of sacred force is not a uniquely European concept. Sigfried Giedion writes of the discovery, in the 1950s in the Cordilleras of Bolivia, of a group of large stones deeply engraved with vulva images (see fig. 6.3). Found covered with moss and vegetation in a high mountain pass, they bear an uncanny resemblance to the thirty-thousand-year-old vulva stones of La Ferrassie, France, although the date of the Bolivian stones has not been set. The Chimane Indians who lived in these Bolivian highlands had been relatively untouched by Western civilization or missionary influence. This place of the vulva stones was a Chimane sacred spot, close to their source of rock salt, which they regarded as closely related to fertility. For the Chimane, salt was synonymous with life and the renewal of human life. They held persistent tribal memories of salt rituals and ceremonies associated with this sacred place of the vulva rocks.

Because many of these vulva iconographs were found together with images of the hunt, they have usually been interpreted simplistically as fertility signs representing animals evoked by the male hunter. Giedion however, calls these ancient vulvas "an obvious symbolic expression of the desire for the perpetuation of the species. No distinction was made in this context between man and animal. To increase and multiply was necessary

FIGURE 6.3 *Boulders from the salt sanctuary of the Chimane Indians in Bolivia, thickly engraved with vulva symbols very much like Paleolithic images found in France.*

(Giedion, 1962, p. 185, figs. 114, 115.)

for the continuation of the human race and for the continuation of the various animal species."[3] Giedion goes on to make the important point that in these primeval times there must have been tremendous loss of life of mothers and infants at birth, and many children did not survive their first years. It is hard for us, from the vantage point of our overpopulated earth, to imagine how significant each new birth would have been to those tiny isolated family groups. These millennia-old vulva symbols must have reflected a complex of attitudes concerning the sacredness and significance of fecundity, attitudes whose emotional significance is difficult for us to absorb. Giedion sees these engraved stones as fertility symbols that possibly played a part in early ritual ceremonies.

Henri Delporte observes that although Paleolithic artists were able to depict animal forms with astonishing skill and verisimilitude, they chose to depict the vulva abstractly. He leaves open the question of whether the vulva images were created as symbolic yet naturalistic depictions of the female body or as concise symbols of the process of creating life. Delporte agrees with Giedion, saying, "The figuration of the vulva reveals . . . a complexity of thought and, at the same time, an initial power of abstraction or an idealization that is astonishing."[4]

Paleolithic artists sometimes integrated their vision of the vulva as a symbol into more complete images of the female body. From a cave at L'Angle-sur-L'Anglin, France, a frieze emerges from the cave wall with three almost life-size female figures, dated circa 17,000–14,000 BCE (see fig. 6.4). Carved into the uneven rock, these powerful figures are surrounded by other carvings of bison, horses, and ibex. The three female forms have neither heads, breasts, arms, nor feet. All emphasis is on their reproductive parts. Giedion comments on the L'Angle frieze: "Had there been a need to represent the entire body, it could easily have been done in the space available. But apparently no such need was felt, and so only the abdomen, the pelvic area, and the vulva have been carved. The entire figure was not important, but only the fragment which stood for the whole."[5]

Another extraordinary rock carving found in 1940 at Le Gabillou, France, dates from the same period as the L'Angle frieze, but at Le Gabillou there is a single female image. Inscribed into the rock face, a naked woman lies spread-legged on her back (see fig. 6.5). Again, neither head nor arms

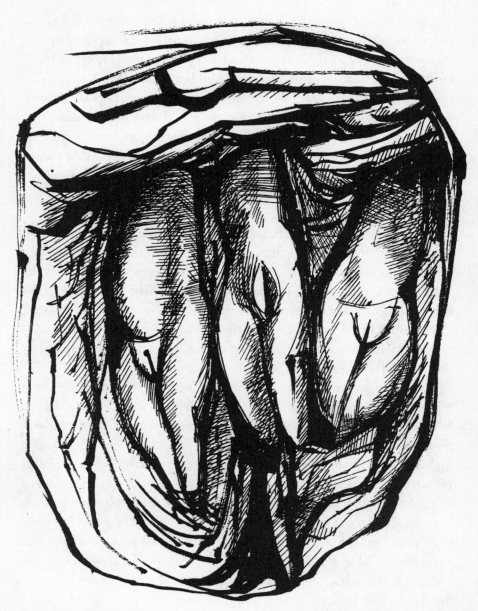

FIGURE 6.4 *Three life-size carved female figures from the cave of Angles-sur-l'Anglin, France. 15,000 to 10,000* BCE. *Musée des Antiquités Nationales.* (Delporte, 1972, p. 89, fig. 49.)

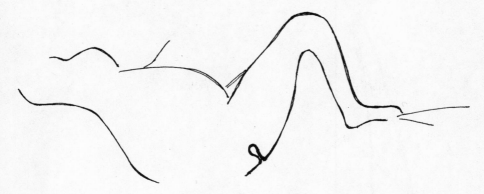

FIGURE 6.5 *The Woman of Le Gabillou, France. Ca. 15,000* BCE.
(Delporte, 1979, p. 86, fig. 46.)

were thought necessary, only the curve of breast and belly, with one leg
bent and the sex explicit. This rock engraving, circa 15,000 BCE, has all the
authority of line of a Matisse drawing.

Alexander Marshack has done research on possible ritual uses of the
vulva images found in Ice Age sites in Europe and has examined great
numbers of these artifacts using "the finest micro- and macro-optical
equipment." After careful analysis, he asserts that some of these female
images were made to be used, that they were often over-marked with
strikes and gashes as if they had been used in ritual. He writes that the
Paleolithic vulva images are

> sometimes associated with the mother goddess or presented as a symbol
> and aspect of her story, sometimes in graves, sometimes associated with
> other symbols. These uses and variations increase our understanding of
> the complex, interrelated nature of the story and take it out of the realm
> of mere sexuality. It is not the anatomic "sexual" organ that is being
> symbolized, but the stories, characters, and processes with which the
> symbol had become associated.[6]

A 15 cm (six-inch) carved piece of antler bone has been found at the cave
of Le Placard, Charente, France, dated 15,000–13,000 BCE (see fig. 6.6).
This bone was carved into a headless elongated torso with spread, trun-
cated legs. Between the legs is a most carefully observed vulva, but the

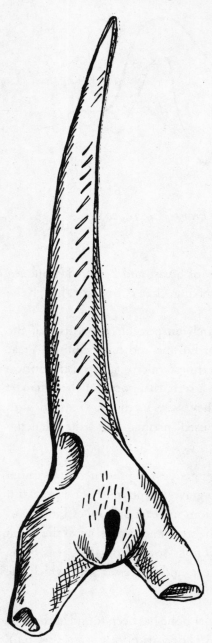

FIGURE 6.6 *A carved and inscribed reindeer bone from Le Placard, France. Possibly an androgynous image. Ca. 20,000* BCE. *Musée des Antiquités Nationales.*
(Delporte, 1979, p. 88, fig. 47; and Marshack, 1972, p. 293–94, figs. 166a,b,c.)

upper part of the body is a phallus. Marija Gimbutas speculates that this artifact "may signify a belief that combining the vulva and phallus in one image strengthens the life force."[7]

Marshack writes with regard to his work on this same antler bone from Le Placard:

> The microscope reveals that this bâton is marked by an extremely fine series of sequential marks made by different points and rhythms, marks which may be notational or otherwise storied [other pieces from Le Placard have notations] . . . some of which were related to a lunar count. Could these, then, be notations related to menstruation or pregnancy, or to a rite related to one or the other? Whatever the interpretation, the forked image . . . served as a sign or symbol of some specialized aspect of the female process and story.[8]

Rawson speculates along the lines of female process and story and proposes that carved bones similar to the artifact from Le Placard may have been ritually employed. Rawson goes a step further than Marshack:

> It seems quite probable—though the more genteel archaeologist may rebel at the suggestion—that the heads of these figures were actually inserted into the vulvas of women or girls in the course of initiations, for example, to 'incorporate' them with the image of the Fertile Mother. Comparable ritual acts are known from, among other regions, Africa and aboriginal India.[9]

One day in 1864 at Laugerie Basse, France, a startled French archaeologist unearthed a small headless bone figurine. The story is told that the discoverer, holding the still dirt-encrusted figure in his hand, spontaneously christened it "La Venus Impudique" (the shameless Venus) (see fig. 6.7). Such is the apocryphal story given to explain the Venus appellation that has clung persistently to the hundreds of Paleolithic female figurines subsequently unearthed in Europe and the former Soviet Union. This first of the discovered Venuses, carved from a bit of mammoth bone, measures about 8 cm (just over three inches) in height and is dated circa 14,000 BCE. Like many cave engravings, she seems to have been conceived and created without head, arms, or feet. It is her sex that rivets attention. We are told that when this figure was first found there was evidence of vivid red ocher

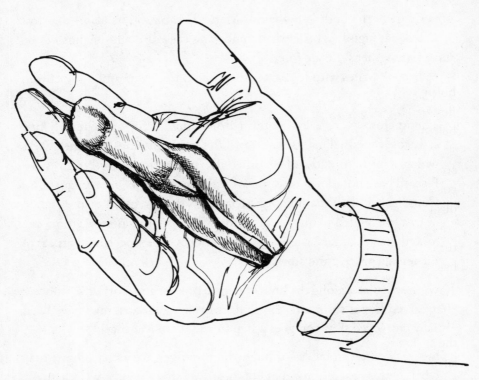

FIGURE 6.7 *The "Shameless Venus" of Laugerie Basse, France. An ivory figure, found in 1864 and dating from about 15,000* BCE. *Musée de l'Homme, Paris.* (Delporte, 1979, p. 55, fig. 21; White, 1986, p. 155, fig. 186.)

pigment smeared and still visible over belly, breasts, and the genital area. No wonder monsieur le professeur was startled.

These figures show the vulva as a forceful symbol. We can only speculate on what these images meant to the women and men who created them. We can accept either Giedion's cautious statement that "they were an obvious symbolic expression of the desire for the perpetuation of the species"[10] or Marshack's view that "we know only that the range of [Paleolithic] female images and the many forms of presentation and use preclude any simple interpretations. The sum of such images implies a time-factored, storied way of thinking."[11]

One of the most spectacular of Paleolithic works of art is the statue known as the Venus Laussel. It was carved into the rock wall of a shelter at Laussel in the valley of the Dordogne in France, an area rich in Paleolithic discoveries. The stone relief carving spans 42 cm (about seventeen inches), relatively large for these figures, and dates from circa 24,000 BCE (see fig. 6.8). This Venus has a mature female shape with an opulent body, full breasted and wide hipped. Her head is turned toward her right arm, which holds aloft what appears to be either a horn or crescent moon. Long, flowing hair covers most of her featureless face. Her left arm rests on her belly with the hand pointing to her genital area.

Marshack notes that the figure's moon/horn was carved with thirteen straight marks and may be more than a simple symbol of fertility: "The count of thirteen is the number of crescent 'horns' that may make up an observational lunar year."[12] He considers it possible , although not proven, "that the 'goddess' with the horn is a forerunner of later Neolithic, agricultural variants. She was the goddess called 'mistress of the animals' [and] had a 'lunar mythology.' "[13]

According to W. I. Thompson, the curved object the woman holds is a crescent moon, which expresses the relation between the moon and woman and that the thirteen incised marks symbolize the phases of the moon from the new moon to the full (in women's mysteries from menstruation to ovulation) or the thirteen lunar months of a year. He writes that "since the people of this period carved innumerable vulvas on the walls of the caves, it is natural to assume that the monthly rhythms of the vulva were closely attended to, and that ovulation was no invisible event but was a subtle tidal pulse that seemed to be drawn by the apparitional light of the full moon."[14]

The Laussel relief, with its unity of horn/moon and vulva, is not an isolated phenomenon of Paleolithic art. Hundreds of other small statues of women, most of them not as well known as the Laussel statue, have been unearthed. They date from 30,000 to 10,000 BCE and have been found in widely separated areas, from Siberia to Spain. Among them are figurines that have similarities to Baubo's gesture or posture.

In recent years in various parts of the former Soviet Union, many Paleolithic figurines have been discovered. One 10 cm (four-inch) female figure was unearthed at Kostenki, a village on the bank of the Don river south of Voronezh in Russia (see fig. 6.9). Carved from a piece of mammoth bone, it shows a woman perched on tiny feet, her head bent forward as if contemplating the plenitude of her full body. It dates from about 25,000 BCE. A similar and more dramatic figure, dating from 27,000 BCE, was found in

FIGURE 6.8 *The "Venus" of Laussel, France. Ca. 20,000* BCE.
Musée d'Aquitaine, Bordeaux.
(Delporte, 1979, p. 61, fig. 25; Marshack, 1972, p. 334, fig. 202a;
and White, 1986, p. 128, fig. 148.)

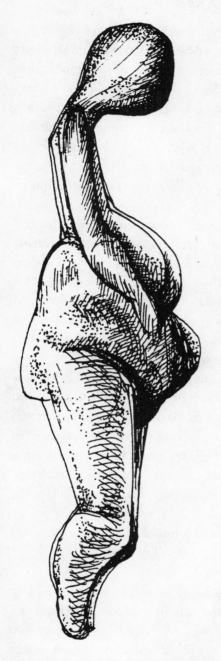

FIGURE 6.9 *A figurine from Kostenki, Russia,
carved from mammoth bone. Ca. 25,000* BCE.
(Delporte, p. 169, fig. 108.)

1922 near Lespugue, France. This tiny but wonderfully opulent figure was found by accident when an archeologist, ending the day with a final thrust of a pickax, unearthed and, sadly, fractured a portion of the figure's front (see figs. 6.10 and 6.11). It is rare indeed to find one of these ancient carvings intact. The Kostenki and Lespugue figurines have survived not only with their heads but also with their feet. Like the Laussel relief carving and like most other Paleolithic figurines with retained heads, however, they are faceless, a condition long considered by archaeologists to be the rule for female images from the Ice Age and perhaps an indication of sacredness or the sign of a deity.

Between 10,000 and 8,000 BCE the great ice sheets and glaciers that had blanketed one third of the earth began to shrink, and the resulting climatic changes forced adjustments in the lives of the small groups of wandering peoples in the Ice Ages. The mammoth and other herds hunted by these people began to disappear, while the weather became more hospitable for the earliest agricultural attempts. Thus a new way of life developed, a new stone age, which we call the Neolithic. In talking so glibly of Paleolithic moving into Neolithic, we are dealing with vast stretches of time, thousands upon thousands of years. Yet it must be stressed that Paleolithic iconography of creation, death, and rebirth persisted while the idiom and archaic symbols of female sexual energy continued—an imagery that was varied but never forgotten. Neolithic symbols of female power have been found on thousands of pots, on sacred objects found in shrines, on amulets, on statuettes, and on objects placed in graves. Thousands of small clay, bone, and stone female effigies have been discovered, and are usually given the name of goddess or earth mother.

But according to Marija Gimbutas it is a mistake to lump together all these Neolithic images and think of them as fertility goddesses:

Fertility is only one among the Goddess's many functions. . . . Earth fertility became a prominent concern only in the food-producing era; hence it is not a primary function of the Goddess and has nothing to do with sexuality. The goddesses were mainly life creators, not Venuses or beauties, and most definitely not wives of male gods. . . . They impersonate Life, Death and Regeneration; they are more than fertility and motherhood.[15]

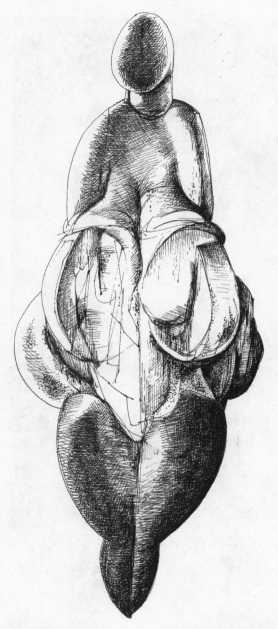

FIGURE 6.10 *Figurine from Lespugue, France, carved from mammoth ivory. Ca. 27,000* BCE. *Musée de l'Homme, Paris.*

(Delporte, 1979, p. 33, fig. 13. Drawing shows the disfiguring damage the original suffered when unearthed in 1922. For a reconstruction, see fig. 6.11.)

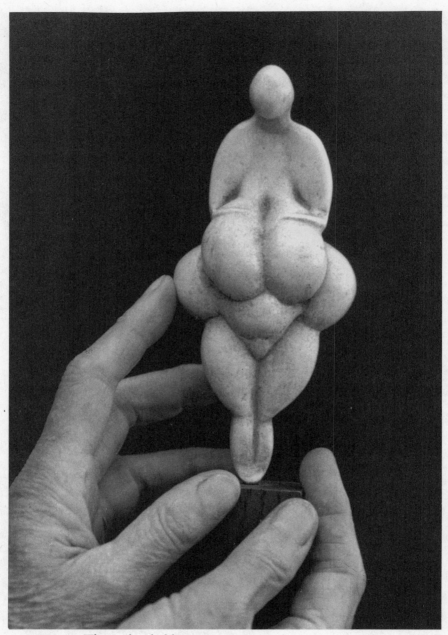

FIGURE 6.11 *The author holding an epoxy copy, from the Louvre, of a reconstruction of the Lespugue figurine shown in fig. 6.10.*
(Photograph by Norma Holt.)

Gimbutas elucidates the myriad forms and symbols that appear in the Neolithic concept of female power and energy. She shows how the vulva continued to be venerated and how the goddess was also seen as a snake, bird, hedgehog, frog, or fish deity. Gimbutas says of the fish that it was often used as a Paleolithic "symbol of becoming . . . associated very early with the vulva."[16] A magnificent Fish Goddess statue was recently found at Lepenski Vir, in Serbia (see fig. 6.12). At this site in 1965–67, Yugoslav archaeologists unearthed detailed evidence of a long-settled Neolithic community perched on a rocky ledge overlooking the Danube at the Iron Gate Gorge. They excavated eight separate levels of methodically planned and architecturally distinctive human habitations. Carbon dating tests showed that this settlement had been occupied for almost a thousand years, from around 5410 to 4610 BCE.[17]

Fifty-four large stone sculptures were found embedded in the floors of these house sites at the side of "altars." Some of the two- or three-foot boulders were egg-shaped and were carved to represent a face; others were images of whole bodies, and still others were incised with abstract designs of graceful arabesques (see fig. 6.13). There is some evidence that one or two of these carved boulders had been placed beside every hearth-altar. One small egg-shaped boulder set beside an altar is an exact image of a vulva, "not as it is normally seen and usually depicted but in a specific physiological state as at the onset of birth with all its anatomical detail."[18] This small vulva stone from the Danube, circa 5275 BCE, shows an unbroken continuity of symbol from the carved rocks found in France, created 24,000 years earlier.

But the Fish Goddess statue found at a different level beside an altar at Lepenski Vir is quite unique; it has no duplicate. Its date is circa 4680 BCE. Carved from a coarse-grained yellow sandstone, she stands about 85 cm (two-and-a-half feet) high. Her head is thrust back, her eyes are wide and staring, and her mouth is loosely parted and drooping, giving her face a fish-like look. Her body, compressed within the boulder shape, has two small round breasts, while her hands hold open her vulva. "Was the Fish Goddess a primeval creatrix in whose power was the renewal of life?"[19] asks Gimbutas, noting the bird-claw shape of the four-fingered hands and the egg shape of the boulder.

Dragoslav Srejović, the chief archaeologist at Lepenski Vir, applies to

FIGURE 6.12 *Photograph of the "Fish Goddess" of Lepenski Vir, in situ, northeastern Serbia. 6595* BCE. *National Museum, Belgrade.* Belgrade University Collection. (Srejović, 1972, p. 85, pl. 24.)

FIGURE 6.13 *Three carved sandstone boulders from Lepenski Vir, northeastern Serbia. 6595* BCE. *National Museum, Belgrade.* (Srejović, 1972, p. 106 #26, pl. 5, #38.)

that extraordinary site these figures: "the distinction of having produced the earliest known sculptures to represent the human head life-size and larger. These are in fact the oldest stone monumental sculptures yet discovered."[20] Srejović is clearly eager to share his enthusiasm over these finds: "These representational sculptures, stylized as they are, seem to be imbued with a strange vitality not to be found in realistic portraiture and make a powerful impression on the beholder."[21] There is evidence of accumulations of bones of red deer, dogs, and boars, as well as great numbers of fish bones found at this riverside settlement; many human bones were also found buried inside the habitation sites. Srejović sees these burials as religious evidence: "It seems therefore, that this religion was primarily concerned with the mysteries of birth and death and that in it the most important place was given to the ancestors who watched over the prosperity of the entire community and preserved the fire on the hearth."[22]

Gimbutas, however, in her analysis of the same material, comes to the conclusion that Lepenski Vir was a sacred settlement where the Fish Goddess was worshipped, but, more significant, that the large number of unbroken animals bones found there indicate ritual sacrifices. "The people's main activities at Lepenski Vir were ritual sacrifices and the carving and engraving of sacred sculptures and cult objects in association with burials." Thus, in Gimbutas's opinion, the Fish Goddess must be seen as "Mistress of Life and Death, a generative womb."[23]

The gesture of this Fish Goddess from the Danube, with her four-fingered bird hands prominently exhibiting her generative symbol, is repeated, with variations, in many other examples of Neolithic art. Two Neolithic statuettes repeat similar poses. The first, a smaller figure made of bone, dates from 4000 BCE and was found in Israel. The head of this figurine is lost, but with hands turned inward and placed above the genital area her gesture echoes the Lepenski Vir figure. The randomly drilled holes were perhaps meant to indicate pubic hair (see fig. 6.14).

Another variant on the same theme comes from Phoenicia and is dated at about 2500 BCE (see fig. 6.15). This small terra-cotta statue from Sidon also has its hands placed below its waist with fingers pointing downward. The eyes, nose, breasts, and navel are carefully incorporated into the design, but no mouth is indicated. This goddess wears an elaborate necklace, whose design repeats the shape of the vulva or vulva covering. The necklace, in Gimbutas's opinion, is often an identifying symbol of the goddess's presence and her regenerative potential.[24]

Other more abstract symbols of a generative goddess focus attention on the vulva. One, a small gold amulet with a crowned head, comes from Israel from a later period, circa 1500–1200 BCE (see fig. 6.16). This incorporates the briefest symbol of a necklace under its chin with all the pertinent iconography of breasts, an indented navel, and a large well-defined vulva,

FIGURE 6.14 *A bone figurine from the Beersheba area, Israel. Ca. 4500–3150* BCE. (Author's drawing made at Israel Museum, Jerusalem, 1986.)

complete with indications of pubic hair. Two marble statues from the Aegean show the same insistent emphasis on the genital area. The older, dating from 2500 BCE, is from one of the Cycladic Islands (see fig. 6.17). Evidently, arms, hands, and legs were considered unnecessary to the central image of the head and torso. The sense of the symbol is amply expressed by breasts and an out-of-proportion vulva. The other statue comes from another Aegean island, Delos, and is dated about 2000 BCE (see fig. 6.18). Made of marble, 23 cm (just over nine inches) high, this stone statue has a compelling and regal stance. With its long slim neck and coronet, it needs no identifying necklace to assert its divinity. Again its genital area is large and explicitly designed.

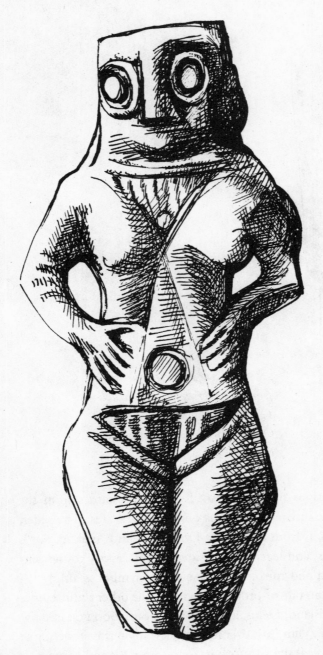

FIGURE 6.15 *A Phoenician terra-cotta. Ca. 2500* BCE. *The Louvre, Paris.*
(Neumann, 1974, pl. 14.)

FIGURE 6.16 *A gold amulet from Tel Baiteglain, Israel.*
Ca. 5000 to 12,000 BCE.
(Author's drawing made at Israel Museum, Jerusalem, 1986.)

These figures with their crowns, their necklaces, their vulvas, and their gestures of epiphany state again and again the theme of feminine sacrality. It would be a mistake, however, to assume that such images are therefore indications of a matriarchy or of women playing revered roles in society. Worship of goddesses does not alone prove this. For example, the intense idolatry of the Virgin Mary in medieval Europe or of the Devi in India does not necessarily indicate that women in those societies had a higher status than men. The denigration of women in everyday life is another matter—beyond the scope of this book. Ironically, in the modern world this disparity is inverted. Parallel to the independence and power being gained by women, their portrayal in the media today has become increasingly obscene. Baubo's gesture, once sacred, is now a centerfold in a porno magazine.

The illustrations for this chapter were chosen from among hundreds of images of prehistoric women available for testimony in the iconographic record. One particular image spoke to me instantly, claiming her place as

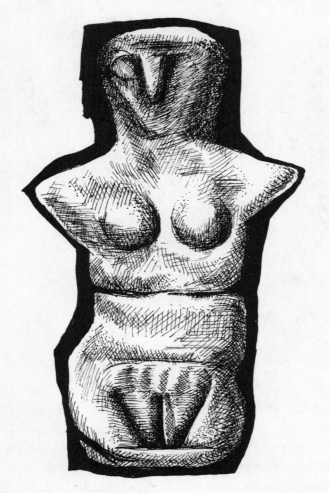

FIGURE 6.17 *Cycladic marble torso and head. 2500* BCE.
British Museum, London.
(Devereux, 1983, p. 77, fig. 15; Neumann, 1963, pl. 23.)

an ancient expression of Baubo. Carved from a tiny piece of mammoth bone, this statue measures just 6.5 cm (a little more than two and a half inches) in height (see fig. 6.19). She was recovered from a site in Siberia, at M'alta near Lake Baikal, where Russian archaeologists have been working since 1928 and where they have made many astonishing discoveries, including carved Paleolithic artifacts that seem to indicate a well-established community of hunters and a society where women may have played im-

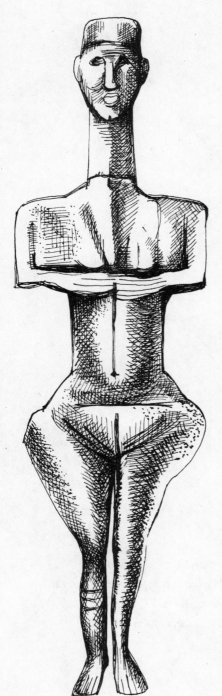

FIGURE 6.18

Marble statue from Delos. 2000 BCE.

(Bossert, 1937, p. 242, pl. 410.)

FIGURE 6.19 *"My Lady of M'alta." Ivory, about 7.5 cm tall, from Siberia. Ca. 12,800* BCE. (Delporte, 1979, p. 198, #24.)

portant and revered roles. Some twenty-seven female figurines have been found at M'alta. All were dug from enclosed hearths, not burial sites, in human habitations where women apparently occupied one side of the living space and men the other, in a very clear and defined manner. The figurines are dated circa 17,000 BCE. These Siberian pieces bear many resemblances to the "Venus" statuettes found in European Paleolithic sites, but with one important difference. A few of the Siberian figures have clearly indicated faces, whereas the European heads are almost always faceless.

This particular figurine, which I have named My Lady of M'alta, has distinct facial features. This is a real woman who gazes out at us from deep-set eyes. Her long nose ends in chiseled nostrils, and her wry mouth seems about to smile. Her arms rest on her belly with hands pointing toward her vulva; her pendant breasts hang like those of a woman who has frequently given suck. She has no feet—perhaps the pointed bottom of the statuette was stuck into soft earth beside the hearth. Or it may be that this type of figurine like the bone carving from Le Placard (see fig. 6.6) was used as a ceremonial tampon to be inserted into the vagina in ritual observances at puberty or before or after birthings—a custom that has been observed by anthropologists among some Eskimo peoples.

My fancy, not my reason, tells me that here I have found Baubo. I do not mean to imply that this strange and wonderful image from thousands of years ago is an actual representation of Baubo. Rather, I look upon her as a "subsidiary image." As Marshack puts it, "The name, the story, and the image of a god, goddess, or spirit lasts through time. But the use, renewal, and reference to the god or goddess is never constant; it is always specialized and limited. It is often partial, performed by word, a saying, a gesture, or through a subsidiary image, a time-factored rite, or by reference to still another character in the story."[25] It is exactly in this way that concepts like Baubo and the "subsidiary image" of her vulva persisted, emerging much later in legends, like the tip of a mythic iceberg whose immensity lies deeply submerged.

CHAPTER SEVEN

In Greece, myth escapes from rituals like a genie from a bottle. Ritual is tied

to gesture, and gestures are limited: what else can you do once you've burned

your offerings, poured your libations, bowed, greased yourself, competed in

races, eaten, copulated? But if the stories start to become independent, to

develop names and relationships, then one day you realize that they have

taken on a life of their own.

—*Roberto Calasso*[1]

Sacred or Profane?

Certain body gestures appear again and again in ancient art; and a few pertaining to women and their activities have become part of our visual vocabulary. Three apply to the imagery of Baubo: upraised arms, Baubo's gesture of *ana-suromai*, and a frog-like squat. All three gestures have gradually acquired both sacred and profane connotations.

The posture of women standing with upraised arms, the gesture of mourning, is very ancient and is understood throughout the Mediterranean area as a sign of reverence for the dead. It is also an ancient gesture

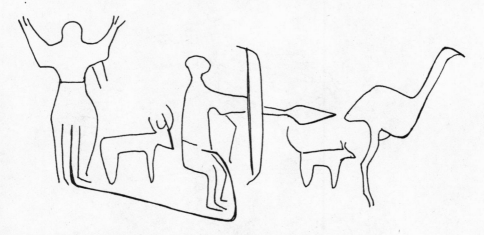

FIGURE 7.1 *Cliff engraving of an ostrich hunt from the Sahara. Tiout, Algeria. Late Paleolithic.*
(Vaufrey, 1937, p. 75, fig. 14.)

signifying the appearance of a divine or supernatural being, an epiphany. The gesture of epiphany is illustrated in a series of rock carvings from the Sahara, discovered in 1910. These carvings on a rocky cliff at Tiout, Algeria, are thought to date from the late Paleolithic. In one of these, a large figure wearing a long gown with tasseled sleeves dominates the scene (see fig. 7.1). It stands with uplifted arms while a small cow-like animal with a circle set between its horns moves in front. A hunter crouches with bow and arrow, his dog between him and an ostrich. The figures are placed in close formation, not quite touching. What shifts this group from an ordinary ostrich hunt into an image of magical significance is the deeply incised line that connects the genital area of the woman to the genital area of the hunter. There can be no doubt that this flowing line was intended to suggest the sexual energy moving between the female and the male hunter.

The woman figure's gesture of upraised arms is important here. In discussing this Saharan engraving, Erich Neumann says that "the 'specific activity' of the upraised arms is unquestionably religious, whether we interpret it as prayer, invocation, or magical conjuring. Primary in all probability is the 'magical significance' of this posture, which was later retained as an attitude of prayer."[2] The same posture of upraised arms found in so many ancient images may personify either a divine being, a blessing,

FIGURE 7.2 *A Sumerian goddess of beasts, birds, and fish. From ancient Larsa in Iraq. Ca. 2000* BCE. *The Louvre, Paris.*
(*Encyclopédie photographique de l'art*, vol. 1, p. 252.)

or simply a greeting between a divinity and a worshipper; but in some archaic cultures it was used to identify a goddess. This seems to be the case on a clay pot from Larsa in Mesopotamia, made circa 2000 BCE. The vase, only 28 cm (eleven inches) high, is decorated with a line-incised drawing of a naked woman with her arms raised in the gesture of the holy presence (see fig. 7.2). Surrounded by fish, a bird, and a turtle, this winged being has bird's claws for feet. Her breasts are small in comparison with her large and well defined vulva. She wears the elaborate horned headdress and necklace of a Sumerian deity. Bird and fish images are repeated on the reverse side of this pot, with a magnificent bull completing the symbols of the animal world ruled by the Bird Goddess. At the Louvre, this treasure from Sumer is entitled simply "Goddess of Fertility and Fecundity."

The standing gesture of epiphany made by a frontally presented naked female is far easier for modern viewers to read as holy than is the posture of a naked woman squatting. With this image our partriarchally conditioned sight falters, and we are likely to turn away in disgust. Margaret Murray, who classifies these frog-like figures as "the Personified Yoni," argues that artistic and cultural difficulties involved in such depictions are largely resolved by the use of the squatting posture, with emphasis placed unequivocally on the image of the genitalia. Murray notes: "In this type beauty of form or features is disregarded, the secondary sexual characters, such as the breasts, are minimized; the whole emphasis is laid on the pudenda."[3] Murray further asserts that "the front view is essential, the genitalia must be exaggerated in size and somewhat distorted in position, and the attitude of the figure may be such as to show the pudenda in a specially marked manner."[4] The most direct way to achieve this graphically is to use the frog or squatting posture. The squat is ubiquitous, occurring in iconography on every continent. Anthropologists have given it the specific title of *hocker* (from the German verb *hocken,* to squat), and in their opinion hockers are frequently representations of the dead.

Two tiny gem seals from Ur (now in Iraq) show hockers and their connections to the underworld (see figs. 7.3 and 0.1, in preface). The seals date from 2800–2470 BCE. One seal shows a naked woman squatting with legs wide apart, so that her vulva becomes the focus, while two scorpions flanking her carefully repeat the curves and actual shape of her vulva. Scorpions in Babylonian culture were ancient symbols of death and the underworld. The second seal from Ur repeats the same squatting posture, but on this seal the underworld aspect of the symbol is even more clearly stated. Here, a flattened dog-like animal guards the naked woman while a scorpion spreads out on her other side, with a long tail that seems to end in a serpent's head. All three animals, dog, scorpion, and serpent, are Babylonian symbols of death and regeneration.

The hocker gesture is frequently seen in archaic art in the time-honored

FIGURE 7.3 *Babylonian cylinder seal from Ur, showing a goddess squatting, flanked by scorpions. Ca. 1500* BCE.
(Devereux, 1983, p. 41; and Mode, *Irdische Frühkulturen*, listed in Neumann, 1974 p. 138, fig. 23.)

posture of the divine as birth-giver. In many parts of the world this is still the normal and accepted birthing posture, only now, belatedly, being revived in Western culture and championed by some women, midwives, and physicians as the easiest and safest position for both mother and baby. One superbly conceived and designed iconograph of the birthing squat comes from the Mogollen culture of the American Southwest. This birth design was painted on a pot made by the Mimbres people who lived between 1000–1200 CE in New Mexico (see fig. 7.4). Very little is known about these prehistoric peoples, but their beautiful black and white painted pots are treasured today. The painted pots were found in graves, placed to cover the face of the corpse. Each pot had a small hole, chipped out of the central area, which appears to have been made only after the pot was completed. Great care was taken so that the hole did not interfere with the painted design, and it has been suggested that these punctures were made so that the sacred spirit of the pot could escape from the grave.

The hocker, the frog, and the toad share a similar squatting posture and have been used since late Paleolithic times as symbols of the feminine as sacred life-giver. Gimbutas illustrates this concept with many examples in *The Language of the Goddess* (1989). One of the earliest, dating from 5000 BCE, combines the uplifted arms gesture of epiphany with a frog-like

FIGURE 7.4 *A birthing scene. Design from a Native American pot of the Mimbres people. Ca. 1000–1200 CE. Peabody Museum, Harvard University.* (Brody, 1977, p. 49, fig. 14.)

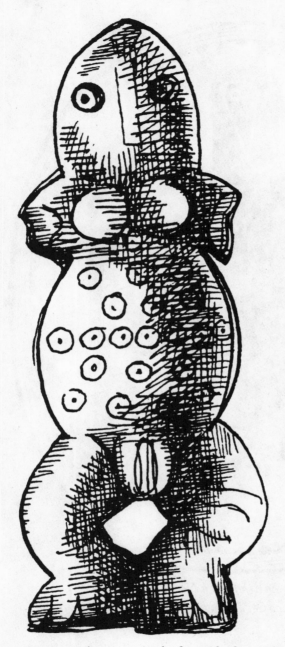

FIGURE 7.5 *A woman in the form of a frog. Eskimo. Ca. 1900* CE.
(Rawson, 1973, p. 127, fig. 72.)

woman's body. That Balkan image has startling similarities to a bone statuette made in our own time by Canadian Eskimos (see fig. 7.5). In the Eskimo carving, the body of a spotted frog is combined with the breasts and the open vulva of a woman's body. The arms are vestigial, and the artist skillfully merges both amphibian and human traits in the head. The Eskimo people often used the frog as a symbol of sexual intercourse. Gimbutas presents yet another "Frog/Woman," which she classifies as one of the "hybrids, symbols of regeneration"[5] in a design from ancient Crete (see fig. 7.6). This vivid frog (akin in design to the Mimbres pot) was painted on an amphora found in the excavations at the Minoan palace at Phaistos, Crete, circa 2000 BCE.

A much later frog-shaped pendant found in the Mesa Verde area of the American Southwest, dated circa 1123 CE, is strikingly similar. This Anasazi ornament is made from layered sections of shell cemented together and is decorated with inlaid bands of fine quality turquoise on the neck, rear legs, and eyes. Found in the grave of an adult woman, this rare frog image may have symbolized rain, fertility, or death beliefs (see fig. 7.7).

Yet another frog image comes from the Neolithic settlement of Haçilar in central Anatolia. This tiny but complete frog-like statue has been identified as a young woman in position of childbirth. Made of light gray burnished clay, the artifact measures only about 7.5 cm (less than three inches), but each articulation of the body is so scrupulously observed and skillfully recorded that the tiny figure evokes magic force (see fig. 7.8). Gimbutas confirms the frog shape of this artifact from Haçilar, calling it a "Great Goddess in the shape of a toad. . . . The mysterious power over life processes which the toad is thought to possess consistently recurs in the consciousness of the European people long after the dissolution of Old Europe."[6] But according to Gimbutas, both frog and toad were death- and life-producing symbols having "their peculiar relationship—even equation—with the uterus of the life-giving, regenerating and transforming Goddess,"[7] but "because the toad was incarnated with the powers of the Goddess of Death and Regeneration, her functions were both to bring death and to restore life."[8]

The frog was revered in Egypt from earliest epochs as Heket, "primordial mother of all existence," and her name was also rendered as Heqit or Hekat. Considered the most ancient of all Egyptian deities, she took the

FIGURE 7.6   *A frog from the Minoan palace of Phaistos. Ca. 2000* BCE.
(Gimbutas, 1989 p. 253, fig. 391.)

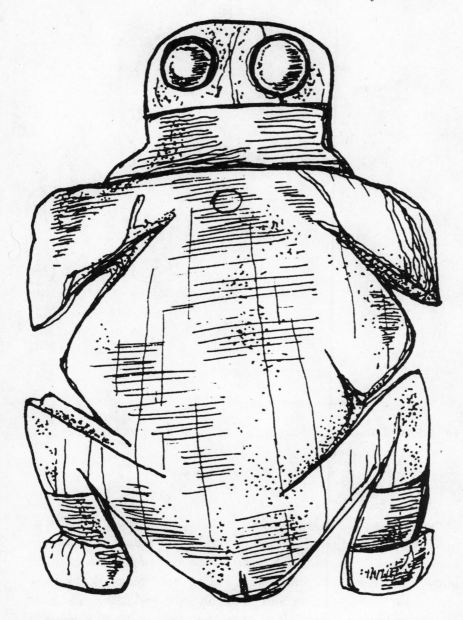

FIGURE 7.7 *An Anasazi frog shell pendant from the Dominguez Ruin in Colorado. Ca. 1123 CE.*

(Anasazi Heritage Center, Dolores, Colorado.)

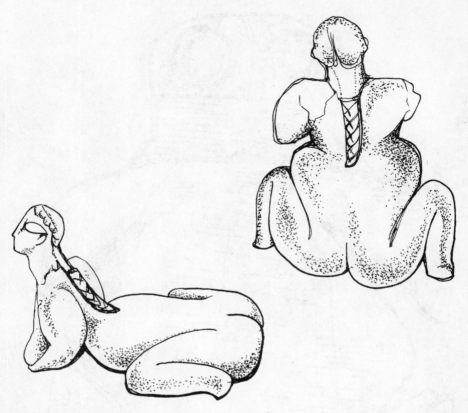

FIGURE 7.8 *Statuette of a young woman in frog posture of birthing. Length 7.5 cm. Haçilar, central Anatolia. Ca. 5400* BCE.

(Gimbutas, 1989, p. 253, fig. 390.1; Mellaart, 1967, p. 481, #201.)

form of frog, toad, or water goddess. She was portrayed as a woman with head of a frog, and the frog was her hieroglyphic sign. The concept of Baubo is thought by many to have originated in Mesopotamia, gradually filtering into Egypt and perhaps via Crete on into Greece. All along this route there are clues that seem to link Baubo with Heket, with images of the squatting frog or toad. The search for traces of Baubo, therefore, includes Ancient Egypt.

At the holy city of Hermopolis, circa 20,000 BCE, Heket was installed in her own temple and worshipped as a frog-headed goddess. She was one of a group of heavenly midwives who assisted each dawn at the birthing of the

FIGURE 7.9 *An Egyptian "magic" knife with Heket, the Frog Goddess. Found in a tomb at Naqada. Ca. 1784–1668* BCE.
(Lacovara, 1988, p. 128, fig. 59.)

sun god. As midwife and as crone, Heket was significant, for she controlled both fecundity and regeneration after death. But, for all her earlier importance, images of her are not easy to find. The problem may be that, as one of the very early goddesses, she did not survive the takeover of the god Amon-Re and his numerous progeny. One frog image from Egypt is now at the Museum of Fine Arts in Boston (see fig. 7.9), where the Egyptian collection includes a small curved ivory amulet identified as a magic knife or wand.[9] Such magic knives were used to delineate protective magic circles around sleeping spaces for protection against illness or snakes and scorpions. They were also placed in tombs to protect the dead from misfortune, and they had special significance as safeguards for women in childbirth.

The Boston "wand" was found in a tomb at Naqada, among grave furnishings placed beside an entombed body. The date given by the museum for this artifact is between 1784 and 1668 BCE, a period when Heket was still greatly revered. Engraved on the polished surface of the ivory is a procession of animals and other images, each an Egyptian symbol of birth and rebirth of particular concern to women. At the far left of the "wand" is an engraved lotus flower, a sacred symbol of creation. Next is a two-legged solar disk that holds an ankh, a life-charm symbol. Then comes a seated jackal figure followed by a composite monster with a winged human head sprouting from its back. Continuing the procession is a lion-like creature and the hippopotamus goddess Taueret (or Taweret), who was the special protector of women in childbirth. Next to Taueret is a large squatting frog representing the goddess Heket. The lineup of protective creatures continues with the gentle cat goddess Bast and ends with another seated feline. Each of these symbols holds before it a knife, the magic symbol of birth and regeneration, repeating the shape of the knife amulet itself.

Heket, the pre-dynastic goddess of the Egyptians, shared many similarities with the early Greek goddess Hecate. Aside from the similarity of their names, both possessed special powers for women, particularly in the areas of birth, both had close ties to the underworld, and both were intimately associated with the image of the frog. Much later, in medieval Europe, such frog personages were metamorphosed into the loathsome toad. They became the familiars of the medieval persecuted witches, and then the toad became equated with the devil, as in "Squat like a Toad, close at the ear of Eve" (*Paradise Lost*, book IV, line 800).

Olender associates Baubo with the frog-toad image as well as with Hecate in her Triple Moon Goddess form, when she combined both witch and magician. He writes: "The hideous look of the batrachian, especially the toad, predisposes the use of these creatures for ancient magical rituals and ceremonies. . . . Ugliness and obscenity and old women were at home with one another, and they show a kinship in antiquity between the demons, monsters, and Hecate and a night-prowling Baubo."[10] Olender completely ignores, however, all aspects of the frog-toad as a symbol of birth and regenerative transformation, the birth-protective role of Hecate, and the nurturing nurse character of both Baubo and Hecate. Nor does he acknowledge the ancient symbology of frog-toad as sacred vulva power, but concentrates instead on the traditional patriarchal view of the old woman as ugly or demonic or as a sinister toad image. This is the same formula heard today, where "You old toad!" remains a term of invective used against women.

Gestures are not always simple to read, for, like symbols, they shift and move about, especially when we attempt to define the sacred and profane aspects of any one particular gesture. In relation to female sexuality, gestures often seem to present two faces. On the dark side, well known and long recorded, the posture of the hocker, the squatter or frog, has traditionally been associated with those hidden body functions we prefer not to mention—defecation, urination, the rigors of birthing—or with nearly forgotten rituals of moon-blood flowing onto the ground.

Wendy Doniger discusses the problem of defining a myth that has outlived its ritual: "And when those myths that are associated with rituals come loose from their ritual moorings, they lose much of their power and relevance."[11] She uses the metaphor of a microscope to illustrate a many-layered approach to myths: "You must constantly change the scale in which you view any particular phenomenon, for there are always at least two levels above and two levels below what you are looking at at any given moment."[12] This hypothetical microscope is useful when shifting the focus between the dark and sacred layers of female gestures.

Doniger's microsocope metaphor applies well to our focus on Baubo squatting in a frog posture and raising her gown before Demeter. Baubo thus may be seen through the lens as a gross, even malign, figure; but, by adjusting the knob, giving a gentle twist, we reach a very different level. The scale then shifts to show an active, dynamic aspect of her gesture. On this new level, we see Baubo making a gesture of change, transformation, and harmony. As Mircea Eliade formulates it: "Now to show something ritually, be it a sign, an object, or an animal, is to declare a sacred presence, to acclaim the miracle of a hierophany."[13]

Hierophany means the showing of the sacred. Keep this firmly in mind as we examine Baubo through the focusing lens of subsequent chapters. She twists in and out of shape, sometimes holy, sometimes pornographic, sometimes a fertility symbol, sometimes a dread Medusa. But always, with a turn of the knob, she comes back into the shape associated with Demeter's trusted nurse and companion, a woman of compassion and power, with her gesture a recognition of body and nature.

CHAPTER EIGHT

A woman in the shape of a monster

a monster in the shape of a woman

the skies are full of them.

—Adrienne Rich[1]

Metamorphosis to Monster

The legend of Demeter and Persephone was a popular subject for Greek artists. A vase made in 450 BCE and now in the National Museum in Athens shows the divine mother and daughter standing face to face, staring deep into each other's eyes (see fig. 8.1). A strongly drawn vertical line separates them. Both women are draped in long, opaque garments. Demeter has a red cloak over her shoulders and wears an ornate crown. She holds three grain stalks whose strong diagonal lines move across into Persephone's space. Persephone carries a lighted torch, symbolic

FIGURE 8.1 *Demeter and Persephone. Detail from an Athenian vase. 450* BCE. *National Museum, Athens.*
(Devambez, 1962, pl. 135.)

FIGURE 8.2 *Seven statuettes of "Baubo" found at Priene, Asia Minor. Fifth century* BCE.

(Halperin, Winkler, and Zeitlin, 1990, p. 110, fig. 3.1; p. 111, figs. 3.2 and 3.3; p. 112, fig. 3.4; p. 113, fig. 3.5; Neumann, 1974, pl. 48; Olender, 1985, p. 4, pl. 1; p. 8, pl. 11; p. 10, pl. 111.)

of her role in the underworld, and pours a libation from a shallow bowl onto the earth. Baubo is not present.

That is the problem. Here is the lacuna, the black hole referred to earlier. Baubo remains an invisible presence in most of classical Greek art. Demeter was frequently portrayed, alone or with her daughter or sometimes with a supporting cast of Olympians, but not with her old faithful servant. There is a striking absence of Iambe/Baubo among the treasury of vase paintings, gemstones, reliefs, and coins. The exceptions are the so-called "Priene Baubos."

Priene, in the fifth century, was a flourishing town on the Ionian coast with an important temple dedicated to Demeter. At the temple site, a team of German archaeologists unearthed a group of curious figurines in the autumn of 1896 (see fig. 8.2; cf. fig. 8.3). Hermann Diels, a renowned classical scholar and part of the team, immediately christened these "Baubos," in reference, he said, to Demeter's old nurse. The Baubo title, impetuously assigned to these particular finds, became firmly affixed when Diels published his articles on the Priene temple discoveries. Although no inscriptions were found with them, these figures continue to be identified with Baubo. Neumann, Picard, Giedion, Devereux, Campbell, and others have published drawings and photographs of the Priene figurines reinforcing Diel's original identification. But other scholars, George Mylonas in particular, have expressed strong doubts and reservations.

These small terra-cottas from Priene are indeed odd creatures. Carl Ruck calls them dwarfs with their faces in their bellies.[2] In each figure the head, belly, and genitals fuse into one amorphous form, and the vulva merges with the chin. Where ears might be expected, some of the statuettes sprout small arms, and while some have mere protuberances for arms, others have no arms at all. Most are naked, their compact bodies set upon sturdy childlike legs. They are generally small, ranging in size from 7.5 to 20.3 cm (three to eight inches). All the figures have carefully arranged coiffures, with luxuriant hair parted in the center, looped back into a chignon, and tied with a ribbon at the top of the head.

There is a curious cuteness about these Priene Baubos with their Kewpie-doll faces. Some hold flowers, some baskets of fruit, others lyres, like charming little dancing girls. They are seductive images of the feminine whose aim is to please. One figurine holds a large torch in each hand,

FIGURE 8.3 *Photograph of Priene Baubo. Antikenmuseum Berlin, Staatliche Museen Preußischer Kulturbesitz.*
(Halperin, Winkler, and Zeitlin, 1990, p. 110, fig. 3.1. Photograph by I. Geske.)

which may indicate a connection to the nocturnal mysteries of Demeter. But for the most part, they have lost any projection of the sacred, or, rather, they are the sacred made infantile and trivialized. Turned into obscene and enchanting dwarfs, they seem to move uneasily between the profane and the pornographic. They are unique in Greek art, quite unlike earlier naked female images, often stark or crude, yet projecting a sense of dignity and authority. The Priene Baubos have undergone a change. They have turned from the holy to the coy.

The disquieting Priene figures raise serious questions in relation to Baubo:

- Is Mylonas correct in his assessment that the Baubo persona was never a participant at the Athenian Eleusinian festival?

- Or, did Baubo indeed play a part at the Mysteries, but a role that remains undisclosed? Just as words spoken at the *Teletai* were considered too holy or too powerful to be revealed, were images likewise proscribed, with the result that not a shred of contemporary evidence linking Baubo to the secret rites has ever been divulged?

- But in that case, why are there no Baubo images from the Thesmophoria, a festival on which such secrecy was not imposed?

A beginning answer may lie in the character of the art objects created by women for women's rituals, which in Greece differed from the art of masculine rituals. Men, as artists, worked with permanent materials, with marble, gold, and silver, with gemstones, fired clay, and metals. Women, never trained as artists, used the impermanent household materials of straw, wood, dough, feathers, and yarn—materials never intended to survive and traditionally accepted as ephemeral. Accordingly, the Baubo images, if created by women for their own rituals, would have disappeared, leaving no traces. We now belatedly recognize the artistic merit of the pieced quilts, samplers, and embroideries designed by our great-great-grandmothers, just as we are now becoming increasingly conscious of ceremonial paintings created by women in many different cultures, of an ephemeral women's art made from string, colored clays, and sand.

Wendy Doniger describes a type of sacred art from Mithali, South India, made by female artists, painters "whose lives are primarily involved in producing human services that leave no permanent trace (with one great exception, of course: children)."[3] The Mithali paintings are designed for specific domestic celebrations and are not made to last. The intricate patterns created with rice powder use natural dyes that soon fade and are swept away after the rituals. "The material traces of ritual art must vanish in order that the mental traces may remain intact forever," explains Doniger. "The rice powder designs are a woman's way of abstracting religious meanings; they are a woman's visual grammar."[4]

Greek women in ancient times used their own "visual grammar" to create sophisticated weavings and embroideries. This women's work, though greatly admired and celebrated in its time, has not survived. The Greek visual art that has survived and is familiar to us reflects basically a male world, a male ideology, created by male artists and craftsmen. No Greek art created by women has come down to us.

Another explanation for the cloak of invisibility that hides Baubo lies in the social conventions of the time, beyond the limitations of artisans' techniques and the transience of available materials. Clearly defined conventions existed that dictated what it was permissible to depict, and nowhere were these strictures or taboos stronger than in the area of sex. Eva Keuls, in her illuminating study of fifth-century Athens, *The Reign of the Phallus*, relies on the "painted history" of vase paintings for evidence of the "phallocracy." She concentrates on images from the second half of the fifth century when Athens was at the height of its imperial power, in the crucial years leading up to the disaster of the Athenian invasion of Syracuse. These were the decades when Athenian society was at a peak of sexual antagonisms, when cultural and artistic attitudes were set and frozen into separate gendered positions: "Pictorial conventions have a significance of their own, although it is not always easy to extract it."[5]

Keuls analyzes the polarization of the sexes and the strong sexual ethic that underlies much of Greek vase painting. She demonstrates, for example, that there were well-observed conventions and limitations about nakedness for each sex in Greek society. Males, both mortal and immortal, were freely portrayed naked; but there were inflexible artistic rules dictating the depiction of the size of the penis. The genitals, whether of a hero like Achilles, lusty Heracles, or the war god Ares, were invariably presented miniaturized, depicted discreetly and as small as a young boy's. Foreigners, however, or slaves or satiric male figures might be shown with extremely large genitals, and fantasy figures, such as satyrs or actors in comedies, were usually depicted with extended penises. In contrast, women (that is, respectable women, and that included goddesses) were invariably shown completely clothed with opaque layers of garments reaching to their toes. The vase painting of Demeter and Persephone (fig. 8.1) faithfully conforms to these artistic conventions of early Greek classical art. It was only about 350 BCE that Praxiteles created his first completely nude statue of the Aphrodite of Cnidus, which profoundly shocked and excited the Greek world.

Praxiteles' masterpiece was rapidly copied and imitated. Up to that date, artistic convention had allowed female nakedness only in the picturing of slave women, foreigners, prostitutes, or the wild maenads. These were the only categories of women who might be shown nude or in explicit sexual postures, and they appeared both in public and in private scenes, with a wide assortment of partners of both sexes, with animals, and with satyrs. The naked, frolicking girls on the beautifully painted pots were *hetairai*, paid companions or slave girls, and these dishes were made by male potters and male painters for men's use at banquets or at the *symposia*, the all-male drinking parties celebrated by Plato.

Classical Greek sexual polarization can be traced in the verbal record as well. The British historian George Thomson writes: "Words are great telltales. They are speaking witnesses to the vanished past."[6] *Aideomai* is one of those "telltale" words in the Greek lexicon that bear witness to the sexual antagonisms of Attic society. *Aideomai* means to be ashamed, but it also means to stand in awe or to fear or to regard with reverence. *Aidoios*, derived from the same root, was an adjective frequently used for women that meant deserving of respect. The neuter noun, *aidoion*, however, was used mostly in the plural for the genitals and particularly the pudenda, *ta aidoia*. Here is fear, awe, shame, reverence, and the pudenda all combined in one word: *aideomai*.

An ancient but persistent visual symbol that "witnesses" all the various meanings of *aideomai* is the legendary Medusa, one of the three Gorgon sisters. Could the Medusa be the transformative link moving from Baubo as sacred vulva, the *aidoios*, to Baubo the scandalous old crone? Were the Priene Baubos an attempt to move away from the Medusa symbol, a way of

FIGURE 8.4 *The Gorgons, sisters of Medusa. Detail of a vase painting found at Eleusis. 670–650* BCE. *Archeological Museum, Athens.*
(Procopiou, 1965, p. 24, pl. 12.)

retaining the comic charm of Baubo the dutiful servant and resisting her metamorphosis into monster? Can this be one clue to Baubo's invisibility? Myths as well as words serve as "speaking witnesses." Medusa's legend in all its variant forms offers interesting supportive evidence for the idea of Medusa as perhaps a transformation of Baubo.

Hesiod in his *Theogony* (776 BCE) refers to the Gorgons as three sisters who dwelt beyond the Ocean in the frontier lands near the Night, the land of the clear-voiced Hesperides, thus setting them far back in the dim beginnings of the world. Hesiod describes two of the trio, Stenno and Euryale, as hideous but immortal, whereas the third sister, Medusa, was mortal, young, and beautiful (see fig. 8.4). He relates how the dark, blue-

FIGURE 8.5 *Perseus slaying Medusa. Detail from a Greek vase painting. Sixth century* BCE. *The Louvre, Paris.*
(Arias and Hirmer, 1962, fig. 36.)

haired Poseidon fell in love with the beautiful Medusa and how in the spring time they lay together in a soft grassy meadow.[7]

This early bucolic story was superseded by a later bloodier folk tale from Argos, which became the official genealogical myth for Athena, newly created municipal goddess of Athens. It is not unusual for ancient myths to be overhauled and refashioned into folktales or sagas intended to instill confidence in new political or religious institutions.

Centuries later, the Athenian writer Apollodorus (born about 180 BCE) reinterpreted the ancient Gorgon tale. In his version Athena was jealous of Medusa's beauty and punished her by turning her into a terrible monster, changing her lovely hair into writhing snakes, giving her a hideous face that petrified (literally, turned to stone) all who looked upon her. In this poet's tale, Athena befriended the Argive hero-prince Perseus and persuaded him to rid the world of this monster for her sake. Athena arranged all the details of this murderous affair, providing Perseus with the dark helmet of invisibility from Hades and a silver sack tasseled with gold to hold Medusa's severed head. Athena actually guided the hand of the prince as he sliced off Medusa's head with a single stroke of his sickle (see fig. 8.5).

Robert Graves offers an interesting pragmatic analysis of the Apollodorus version. He suggests that the Medusa legend was developed to account for the assaults of the Achaean against the power of the earlier ruling Triple Goddess, that this tale was created to give authenticity and glory to the Argives and their hero, Perseus. Graves sees Perseus as a leader of an expeditionary force sent to conquer Libya, a rich country ruled by Medusa, a mighty queen, who was deified in the ancient Libyan goddess Neith. Neith was one of the oldest of Egyptian goddesses and was Mother of Gods. Perseus fought this powerful queen, decapitated her, and returned home in triumph with her head a trophy in a sack, which he then ceremoniously buried in the Argos marketplace. Graves also suggests that Perseus may have returned not with the queen's head but with her sacred mask, the emblem of the goddess's power.

> This must record an Argive conquest of Libya, the suppression there of the matriarchal system, and the violation of the goddess Neith's mysteries. The burial of the head in the market place suggests that sacred relics were locked in a chest there, with a prophylactic mask placed above them, to discourage municipal diggers from disturbing the magic.[8]

Athena had become firmly established by the fifth century BCE as the official municipal goddess of Athens. Her birth and her persona implied that all ties with the earlier great Earth Mother goddesses had been broken. She was born not from a female deity but directly out of the head of her father, Zeus. She became an asexual goddess and was usually depicted in her warrior guise. "For Athena has lost her female connectedness. Although she is important in the Greek pantheon, it is as one who serves the philosophy of the patriarchy. If she is autonomous, it is with concomitant loss of her sexuality."[9] She carried a long spear, a great crested helmet, and a large round shield and was always shown wearing her aegis, a breastplate originally made of goatskin with thickly fringed edges (see fig. 8.6). The aegis was the skin of Medusa, "which Athena herself had stripped off her victim in order to turn it into a breastplate. The snakes which adorned the aegis like a fringe were Medusa's hair."[10]

Many superstitions surrounded the aegis. It was a badge of divine power, considered so essential to sovereignty that no one, not even Zeus

FIGURE 8.6 *Athena in her glory, wearing her Medusa Aegis. Detail from a Greek vase painting. Ca. 530–515* BCE. *Berlin Museum.* (Arias and Hirmer, 1962, pl. 84.)

himself, could rule without it. The blood of Medusa's snaky locks was believed to have magic properties that could create as well as destroy. "The first drop (as Euripides describes it in *Ion*) from the snakes of Medusa's head, was poisonous, and it brought instant death; the second, from Medusa's veins, brought rebirth and life: 'Two blood-drops that the dying Gorgon shed. One medicines all disease, and one is death.'"[11]

Closer to our time, the English poet Shelley emphasized the death power of Medusa:

> Its horror and its beauty are divine.
>
> .   .   .   .
>
> Yet it is less the horror than the grace
> Which turns the gazer's spirit into stone,
>
> .   .   .   .
>
> A woman's countenance, with serpent locks,
> Gazing into death or Heaven from those wet rocks.[12]

It is also possible that the death-giving drop of Medusa's blood was a transposed and distorted memory of the moon-blood that gave women power and that Medusa's terrible mask was a reflection of menstrual taboos imposed much later. In many cultures today, superstitions still hold that the look of a menstruating woman can destroy a man or turn him to stone or, at the least, contaminate food and endanger hunting.

The tale of Perseus slaying Medusa appeared at a comparatively late date in Greek legend. Earlier iconographic evidence suggests that the Medusa/Gorgon myth was of greater antiquity. One Medusa image found on a pot from the Aegean island of Melos has been dated circa 1500 BCE (see fig. 8.7). This stylized portrait is complete with wings, fangs, and three-clawed extremities. Marija Gimbutas identifies the two black circles above the Medusa as breasts, commenting, "The early Gorgon was a potent Goddess dealing with life and death, not the later Indo-European monster to be slain by heroes such as Perseus."[13]

By the seventh century BCE in Greece, images of Medusa had become popular talismans intended to protect the viewer from evil. By this time, the Gorgon image was frequently placed on temple pediments, the rooftops of private and public buildings, baking ovens, warriors' shields, individual seals, and on the coins of city-states—wherever protection was needed against harmful or malevolent spirits. A plate from the island of Rhodes dating from the end of the seventh century shows Medusa wearing her Gorgon mask with its characteristic snaky locks, a wide-mouthed grimace with extended tongue, and glaring eyes (see fig. 8.8). Her body is that of an active winged deity. She grasps two birds in the gesture of archaic *Potnia Theron*, the mistress of the wild things. Full breasted, her skirt flung

FIGURE 8.7 *Gorgon/Medusa figure, on a pot from the Aegean island of Melos. Ca. 1500* BCE. *British Museum, London.*
(Gimbutas, 1989, p. 208, fig. 328.)

open by her vigorous open-legged stride, she echoes the posture of a still more ancient Sumerian seal image of the warrior-like Ishtar, the beloved goddess of Babylonia.

By the fifth century BCE in Greece, Medusa's mask was isolated as the quintessential icon of *aideomai,* of fear and shame, with only a faint trace of reverence still clinging to her. For Greek women had by this time come to be regarded as inherently flawed beings, obviously inferior to men, and Medusa had come to represent the sum total of male fears about the power and dangers of female sexuality. "The myth of Medusa," according to Page DuBois, "is a myth of fear of women, fear of their archaism, their self-sufficiency, their buried power."[14]

In his *Méduse,* Jean Claire links Medusa and Baubo, seeing them as twin

FIGURE 8.8   *A winged Medusa. Design on a plate from the Island of Rhodes. Late seventh century* BCE. *British Museum, London.*
(Arias and Hirmer, 1962, fig. 29; Neumann, 1974, pl. 132B.)

embodiments of female sexual power. In his analysis, Baubo and Medusa symbolize the same part of the female body, just as they utilize the same aspects of female power. Claire also uses the name "Gorgo," identifying it as "vulva visualized as a face, or even better, as a face in the shape of a vulva. Baubo, by contrast, is the face sexualized, a face made into a vagina, genitalia humanized by being made into a face."[15]

Gorgo recalls us to the primeval mother, who is always available to us and to whom all questions of return mean death; Baubo is the opening of the future, the reiterated promise of procreation that is stronger than widowhood or any sort of despair. Medusa is also a dismembered body, whose head and sex have been set apart by taboo and who therefore must be continually dismembered, time and again, to prevent anyone from falling under her spell. Baubo is an entity, complete in herself, a replete body, who, by joking, is reduced to the semblance of her pudenda, but whose totality convinces us of the innocence of her disguise.[16]

Claire notes that Freud saw nothing innocent in either Medusa or her counterpart, Baubo, and that Freud associated Gorgo's huge distended mouth with deeply ingrained masculine adolescent fears of the maternal genitals, the snaky locks with childhood's forbidden glances at maternal pubic hair, while her bared teeth were the toothed vaginas symbolic of male fears of castration, the Vagina Dentata. Claire has a different interpretation of the relation among these symbols:

Medusa and Baubo are both embodiments of the female genitalia and thus play corresponding roles between the male and the female sexes. But whereas Medusa shuts off the road of the maternal for the young man after he has reached puberty, Baubo's role is to console and reassure the young woman at puberty, when she is faced with the anguish of motherhood. Baubo and Gorgo are both incarnations of the same organ. . . . Gorgo is the maternal vulva, which may be desired by the other sex but whose intrinsic womb function asserts itself as a taboo. Baubo, the same symbol of female sex in all its obscene female provocation, here serves as a reminder of woman's essential function . . . that of procreation. Both of them are essentially symbols of the completed signs of maturity which permit the order of the world to re-establish and perpetuate itself.[17]

Baubo and Medusa are mythic figures who emerge, sometimes as mediators, sometimes as transformers. They are always involved in the feminine transitional experiences of puberty, menarche, and birthing and in those crucial stages of life for both sexes that are perceived as passages in and out of darkness. They are mythic images bridging physical reality and metaphysical beliefs.

CHAPTER TEN

And I saw a woman sit upon a scarlet-coloured beast, full of names of

blasphemy, having seven heads and ten horns. And the woman was arrayed

in purple and scarlet colour, and decked with gold and precious stones and

pearls, having a golden cup in her hand full of abominations and filthiness

of her fornication: And upon her forehead was a name written, MYSTERY,

BABYLON THE GREAT, THE MOTHER OF HARLOTS AND ABOMINATIONS OF

THE EARTH.

—*Revelation 17:3–5*

Baubo Meets Her Dark Sisters

The joyous fertility rituals of Isis/Baubo continued to be celebrated throughout the Roman Empire until the fourth century CE, when Judeo-Christian dogmas became dominant. Then Baubo was severed from Isis, with Isis reduced to a purely maternal role. Isis, portrayed with her son Horus on her lap, gradually became absorbed into the legend and imagery of the Virgin Mary and into later Madonna cults. And so began Baubo's bitter progression from sacred ritual to emblem of contempt, from a companion of Demeter and Isis to a victim of the Inquisition. Baubo's image

Black Sea and the Sea of Azov, encouraging active cultural and religious interchanges.

Herodotus told of his travels among the Scythians in 450 BCE, reporting with some surprise that the Scythians were not all horse-breeding nomads, but that some whom he called Callippidae, a Greco-Scythian race, sowed and ate corn, onions, garlic, millet, and lentils. Herodotus also reported that on a narrow spit of land that he identified as Cape Hippolaus stood a temple dedicated to Demeter, where she was worshipped as a corn goddess.[3]

In 1864–68, Russian archaeologists excavated a group of royal Scythian tombs at Taman, where four separate burial crypts were uncovered. One crypt had a picture of Demeter painted on the ceiling, suggesting that it was a tomb of a priestess of the goddess. Three golden plaques depicting dancers were found in this crypt, with other gold and jewels mixed among the bones of a woman. The tiny dancers measure less than two inches in length, with the smallest one just 3.5 cm (one and three-eighths inches). The dancers are bare-breasted, wearing *polos* (ceremonial crowns) upon their heads and lifting short gathered skirts. Each plaque is pierced with a number of holes, suggesting that they were embellishments, sewn like spangles onto the robe of the priestess (see fig. 9.1).

These charming dancers are not actually identified as Baubo by the Russian archaeologists.[4] They identify them as dancers who performed at festivals of Demeter. But it is possible that the strictures of Eleusis and the taboos against portraying Baubo did not apply in this far-off outpost of Greek culture, and that in these decorative golden spangles we finally have fourth-century images of Iambe/Baubo. They are images without distortion, women no longer hiding behind the mask of Medusa or the coyness of the Prienes or clothed in the buffoonery of the old crone on the bridge at Eleusis. These tiny figures of gold, retrieved from a Crimean temple grave, are curiously similar to other Baubo-like statuettes unearthed from desert sands in western Egypt, which date from the post-Hellenistic period of about 300 CE.

The Hellenistic period is usually defined as commencing with the death of Alexander in 323 BCE and ending with the suicide of Cleopatra and the Roman conquest of Egypt in 30 CE. A vast and cosmopolitan empire

FIGURE 9.1 *Three "Baubo" dancers. Gold ornaments from the Scythian tomb of a priestess of Demeter. Crimea. Late fourth century* BCE. *Metropolitan Museum of Art, New York, 1975.*
(*From the Lands of the Scythians*, pl. 9.)

evolved during this era. Hellenistic culture was quite different from those of the smaller embattled mainland Greek city-states of the fourth and fifth centuries. A great deal of written and graphic material that has survived from the Hellenistic world reveals a new kind of society, in contrast to the Attic world. Women's lives, in particular, were transformed by influences from the east, Egypt, and Italy. In Hellenistic cities, women moved with comparative freedom outside their homes. They walked the city streets unattended. They came to public ceremonies and took part freely in a wide assortment of state religious rituals. This was also a time when many new as well as ancient religious rituals made their appearance from the East and from Egypt and merged with local cults as well as with the old established forms of Attic religion.

A great number of Hellenistic artifacts were collected in Egypt by the French physician Daniel Marc Fouquet, who first visited Cairo in 1880. Fouquet became fascinated by the land and remained there for the next thirty years, gradually acquiring more and more Hellenistic art objects. Two handsome volumes describing Fouquet's collection were published in France in 1911 and 1921 by the art historian Paul Perdrizet. His work focused new interest on various images in the spirit of Iambe/Baubo. Perdrizet illustrated and discussed two charming standing figures of Hathor or Aphrodite or the so-called Baubo (see fig. 9.2). These sandal-clad figures gracefully face front, performing their ritual gesture of *ana-suromai*. They wear full-length gowns and elaborate ceremonial headdresses partially covering their long dark curls. Tranquil smiles flicker over their mouths as they lift their gowns. Perdrizet remarks that "whatever they are doing, this gesture is not, no matter what is said, a simple obscenity."[5] These statuettes have an engaging spontaneity that reflects the Hellenistic interest in naturalism and an acceptance of human differences and character. Their charm lies in the combination of the trivial or the everyday with the divine, in contrast with Attic art of the epic or ideal.

One fine example of the statues in the Perdrizet volumes represents a serene, smiling Isis seated in a Baubo posture on an upturned harvest basket (see fig. 9.3). The gown is hitched up, proudly revealing her primary role as the fecund source or dispenser of the fruits of earth and life. Yet this *is* a goddess; her wig, her necklace, and the *polos* or crown on her head, make that clear. Whether called Isis or Baubo, this is an agrarian goddess. Perdrizet sees this small figure as possibly celebrating female rituals similar to those that took place during the Thesmophoria: "Her unconscious immodesty should not surprise, because here the agrarian Isis is actually setting the example, without false shame, for her worshippers."[6]

Isis, with Baubo as her alter ego, was at the center of some of the popular new religious cults. Under Roman rule, the worship of Isis absorbed some earlier Hathor cults and continued to include official priestesses and priests, and many of her joyous and elaborate rituals spread throughout the

FIGURE 9.2 *Two terra-cotta statues of Baubo/Isis. Alexandria, Egypt. Ca. third-second century* BCE.
(Perdrizet, 1921, p. 55, pl. V.)

FIGURE 9.3 *Isis seated upon a harvest basket. Alexandria, Egypt.*
(Perdrizet, 1921, p. 128.)

Hellenistic world. The name Isis became synonymous with the black soil of Egypt that was watered annually by the Nile and where the goddess Isis had long been worshipped as a symbol of the fecundity of plants, animals, and humans. Isis came to personify the female part of nature, of everything concerned with the production of other beings. In the decades before Christianity, and afterwards, Isis synthesized qualities of many other local deities: Hathor, Aphrodite, Minerva, Ceres, Baubo, and, in particular, Demeter.

Isis/Baubo/Demeter was an exceedingly popular divinity. From the large number of Hellenistic figurines of the goddess that have been recovered from the soil of Egypt and southern Italy, it can be assumed that these were mass-produced items. Made of bronze or terra-cotta, they were probably used by the populace as ex-votos (devotional or votive offerings) or as tomb offerings. Often their dates and provenance cannot be fixed because by the late nineteenth century such artifacts frequently appeared in the markets of Cairo and Alexandria, sold by peasants who had dug them up in their fields.

Another provocative terra-cotta, found in southern Italy in the early nineteenth century, and long the subject of controversy among scholars, has frequently been linked to Baubo. Picard pointed out that this is not Greek but rather an Italian artifact, which he classifies as a cult figure of Isis. Neumann agrees with this identification but connects the statue with Baubo's performance before Demeter. Devereaux titles this terra-cotta simply "Baubo" (see fig. 9.4).

Whether Isis or Baubo, this artless little figure astride a large pregnant sow conjures up many curious ritualistic meanings. The right leg is in an extended position so that her vulva is unambiguously presented. She carries an object in her left arm that is difficult to identify. Is it a writing slate? Is it some sort of harvest basket? Is it a mirror? Neumann calls it a "mystical ladder."[7] Nor Hall writes: "This ladder-of-the-soul permits the initiate to go back and forth from the desirous mud realm of Baubo (her husband tended pigs) to the transcendent starry heaven of Venus. Women's worship connects the highest with the lowest, the maculate and the immaculate."[8] Perdrizet states unequivocally that the figure holds a musical instrument called the sistrum, which appears frequently in conjunction with imagery of Isis.[9]

FIGURE 9.4 *Baubo upon a sow. Southern Italy.*
(Neumann, 1974, p. 140, fig. 25; and Devereux, 1983, p. 75, fig. 14.)

Keuls describes this same statuette as "a woman in the childbearing position. . . . This scheme is not intended as erotic or obscene; it celebrates birth."[10] She observes that the Greek word for pig, *khoiros*, was also the commonplace for female sex organs, particularly the vagina. Keuls points out that pigs have always been associated with Demeter and that pig sacrifices were part of the rituals, especially at the Thesmophoria, where suckling pigs were sacrificed by women celebrants during part of the festival.[11] Gimbutas reminds us that the sow is a symbol of fecundity, of the Pregnant Goddess, a concept that has roots going far back in antiquity. The sow's "fast-growing, rounded body was probably allegorical of seed and field fertility, and its condition must have been regarded as magically influencing the crops."[12]

The potent symbolism of Baubo and sow has persisted well into our era. Goethe employed this very image in his Walpurgisnacht scene in Faust:

> The venerable Baubo now
> Comes riding on her farrow-sow.
> Then honour be where honour's due:
> Dame Baubo up, and lead the crew!
> With a tough old sow, a mother as well,
> She'd marshal witches or shades of hell.[13]

Here is Baubo/Isis, once a symbol of magical fertility, now transformed into Baubo the witch on the sow, an image of feminine pollution, lust, and evil. It is possible that Goethe saw this very statuette displayed in an Italian museum and that the vision remained with him, later appearing in the Walpurgisnacht as Baubo on a farrow sow consorting with her wild companions. In this new witch role she is the guardian of hell, quite severed from her antecedent, gentle Isis.

These Hellenistic images so frequently intertwined with animals derive from ancient traditions in which the sacred was worshipped in both animal and human form as one and the same. In Egypt, in particular, all divinities had dual manifestations in animal and human shape. Egyptian religion made no distinction among Hathor in her cat, cow, and lion forms; the divine Taueret was worshipped as a hippopotamus, Horus as hawk, or Ptah as bull. It may be that the two standing Baubo-like statuettes shown in figure 9.2 are representations of the women who performed ritual gestures of *ana-suromai* before the great god Ptah in his bull aspect.

The spirit of Baubo was clearly present in the worship of the Egyptian bull god. It had long been the custom of the Egyptians at the holy city of Memphis to tend and worship a living bull as a sacred animal. Each one of these holy bulls was given the name Apis and was thought to be the reincarnation of the supreme god Ptah. Each subsequent Apis was called "the renewal of Ptah's life." Further,

> As long as he lived, Apis was daintily fed in the temple which the kings had built for him in Memphis opposite the temple of Ptah. Every day at a fixed hour he was let loose in the courtyard attached to his temple, and the spectacle of his frolics attracted crowds of the devout. It also drew the merely curious; for a visit to the sacred animals was a great attraction to the tourists who were so numerous in Egypt during the Greco-Roman era.[14]

Diodorus was one of those tourists. A celebrated Greek historian, he came to Egypt in 60 BCE and reported on the rituals at the temple of Apis in Memphis: "For the first forty days after the installation of a new Apis, women are permitted into the temple to see the bull face to face. They come and stand before him, tucking up their gowns"(see fig. 9.5).[15] Perdrizet comments:

> It is apparent that the women uncover themselves before Apis in order to receive from him a divine influx in the part of their bodies that they present to him. Ancient folklore has, sometimes, strange ideas about conception: thus it is a belief generally understood that twins can be conceived by the wind. These beliefs, I suppose, are primitive survivals of primitive folklore, that the child is not the result of human copulation. If the women of Memphis do not believe that Apis can make them fecund, I cannot explain what they are demanding from this singular festivity. No matter what is said, it is not a matter of pure obscenity, but rather naturalistic rites which had their beginnings in the soil of antiquity.[16]

Baubo as a dancing Scythian priestess of Demeter, Baubo/Isis as an agrarian goddess, Baubo on her sow, Baubo lifting her gown before the

FIGURE 9.5 *Women worshipping the sacred bull Apis at the temple of Memphis, Egypt. The goddess Isis, on the left, appears to be protecting the sacred animal with her winged arms. Linoleum print by W. M. L., inspired by a statue of Apis and Isis. Ca. sixth century* BCE. *The Louvre, Paris.* (*Encyclopédie photographique de l'art,* vol. 1, p. 123.)

holy Apis of Memphis—all these were images connected in one way or another with sacred rituals, with concepts of fertility and transformative regeneration. They were certainly never intended as obscenities. But there are some other images in the Fouquet collection that encourage a more ambiguous reading. Perdrizet distinguished between the elegant and playful Memphis-type figurines and other statuettes that included drunken and erotic figures, but he cautioned against assuming that all such images were erotic in intent. He suggested that they may have been intended as ex-votos, used as offerings for a girl's recovery from illness or for the desired birth of a daughter. He referred in this respect to a category of little naked squatting female statuettes with barely nubile breasts and small childlike limbs. One figure sits with heels together, holding a bunch of grapes and a quince or a pomegranate, a crown resting on the head. Another plausible explanation for these childish squatting statuettes that Perdrizet does not consider is that they were associated with rituals for a girl's first menses.

A curious visual analog connects these Hellenistic child figures and similar ones created nearer our own time by Eskimo carvers. Both sets of figures suggest themselves as images of transformation, of the movement from one stage of life to another. One Eskimo figure from Kodiak Island, Alaska, is carved from walrus ivory and is adorned with small bright blue glass beads. This was not a toy or plaything, nor was it meant to have erotic connotations. Such ivory images represented the soul of a female ancestor, and young girls received them as important gifts conveying the strength of their tribal forebears. They were sacred family objects passed on after marriage and after the birth of a female child, thus perpetuating the feminine sacred traditions of transformation.

Another Baubo-related matter of transformation in Attic Greek culture brings before us one of the most curious and lurid images of all Greek mythology, the Eye or Evil Eye. Now, the Eye was a symbol of great antiquity. In *The Language of the Goddess*, Gimbutas shows how the Eye, when combined with snakes and bees or vulvas, was associated in ancient Neolithic goddess iconography with ideas of creation and regeneration. But then the Greeks at the height of Attic culture began to lose some of those earlier concepts and linked the Eye to the image of Medusa (or Gorgo). The Eye became the Evil Eye with a message of malignant force. In the eleventh book of the *Iliad*, Homer describes the Gorgon head set like a crown in the center of Agamemnon's great bronze shield. He describes her as grim of aspect, glaring fiercely, while all about her circle fear and panic. The Greek word for the Evil Eye was *baskanos*, or the bewitcher. A *baskanos* could spoil all kinds of life, crops, animals, or humans. And the ultimate *baskanos* was Medusa with her deathly stare. A single drop of blood from her snaky locks or one glance from her dreaded eyes meant death. Figure 9.6 shows an Eye-Medusa design from a Greek dish, circa fifth century BCE. The design combines a group of potent symbols of death and regeneration. A grimacing Medusa is surrounded by two large and fierce Evil Eyes. Two small birds fly between the eye symbols, while two butterflies spread their wings beneath the dish handles. But note that counterbalancing the upper fluttering birds on the bottom pair of eyes is a small dark shape that can be read as a nose or a vulva.

Two playful Baubo/Eye images are found in the Fouquet collection (see fig. 9.7). The first is from the handle of a clay pot. On this fragment, a naked woman wearing a *polos* of the goddess sits astride a great Eye with

FIGURE 9.6 *Design on the base of a Greek cup found in Sicily. It combines the symbols of Medusa and the Evil Eye. Note the butterfly images of regeneration at the handles. Ca. fifth century* BCE.
(Procopiou, 1965, p. 17.)

her legs spread in the posture of Baubo on her sow (see fig. 9.4). Perdrizet interprets this combining of eye and vulva as an attempt to weaken or ward off the Evil Eye, and he identifies the woman as Baubo, thus combining the apotropaic theme of protection with that of fertility. A second, better-preserved Eye/Baubo terra-cotta (see fig. 9.8) portrays a childlike female who is squatting in a frog posture. Traces of bright paint remain in some places on the terra-cotta. Her green gown is tucked up high above her knees, revealing a dark painted pubis. A goddess necklace hangs between her breasts. She holds a red *situla*, the musical instrument associated with Isis rituals, and her opulent flower-shaped crown has three separate tiers, on the topmost tier a centrally placed large Eye.

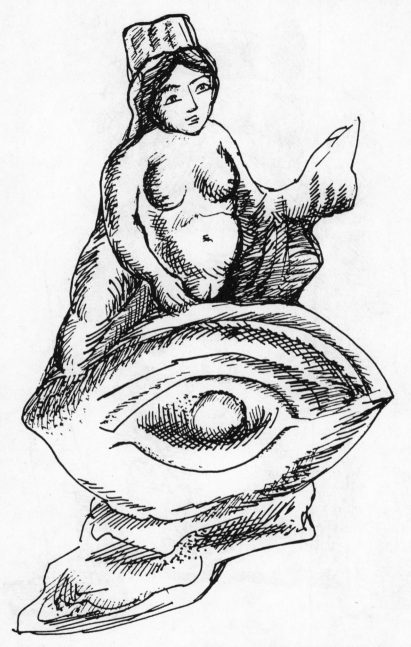

FIGURE 9.7 *Hellenistic terra-cotta figure, perhaps the handle of a pot or lamp. First–second century* CE.
(Perdrizet, 1921, p. 124.)

FIGURE 9.8 *Another terra-cotta figure that links Baubo with the Eye symbol. First–second century* CE.

(Perdrizet, 1921, p. 122, #338; pl. lxxxii)

Although these two Hellenistic images have charm, they are disconcerting in their combination of visual symbols that today we usually keep in separate compartments. In his book on Medusa, Claire observes that

Baubo could be a vulva made into an eye, while Gorgo [i.e., Medusa] is an eye made into a vulva. Both of them, being creatures of the vulva, tend toward those things which are strange, i.e.: the one-eyed, those places and dwellings of creatures or of human beings whose appearance is upsetting, disquieting to those things that alert or divert. In this manner, their nature bears witness to a displacement of functions—an eye for a vulva, or a vulva for an eye. . . . For better or for worse, they are a kind of sacred go-between.[17]

This quality of the "sacred go-betweens," which is the metamorphic essence of Baubo and Medusa, underscores the fundamental ambivalence of their functions. They are two faces of the same phenomenon, whose resemblances are greater than their differences. Medusa and Baubo are both transformative figures that use the Eye, sometimes in its ancient regenerative symbolism and sometimes as the Evil Eye, keeping dire spirits at bay.

The early Christian Church absorbed much of this pagan symbolism, and as old metaphors were transformed, new symbols emerged. Baubo as vulva and Medusa as Eye became equated with the Evil Eye shorn of all concepts of fertility, but retaining some traces of protection. As deeply rooted Judeo-Christian fear of the female came to prevail, other ancient fears of woman's sexual energy as a dangerous pollutant were also incorporated into dogma and popular beliefs. Thus the prevailing symbol of the female became Eve, she who was the bent rib of Adam. And Eve, like Pandora, had brought evil to the earth. Baubo with her positive sexual power had to be banished from the earth or placed among the world of demons and witches. The patriarchy, whether pagan or Christian, came to share an obsessive concern over woman's "lust." This prurient concern gave birth not only to a suppression of imagery but to an intolerance of female sexuality that eventually grew into the monstrous slaughter of women as witches and whores of the devil.

CHAPTER NINE

Whenever you wake, you will hear entering

The song of meanings, a melody of green;

The image of a legendary woman

Dancing among her mercies, in essence emerging

Female to leap into the dragon-throning sea. . . .

—Muriel Rukeyser[1]

The Transformer Transformed

A lucky archaeological find made in 1865 presents us with a dancing Baubo, lifting her short skirt as she moves on tip-toe into "the dragon-throning sea." The figurine was found far distant from Athens, in a tomb on the Taman Peninsula on the eastern shore of the Bosporus, and is thought to date from the fourth century BCE.[2] By this date, areas of the Crimea had long been settled by Scythian nomad tribes, and there were Greco-Scythian trading stations at many places along the shore of the was never lost, only twisted out of shape. The frank and proud personification of female sexual energy, once an integral part of Hellenistic Isis/Baubo worship, was not compatible with the doctrines of the early Christian Church. Christian theology, with its complex synthesis of Syrian, Hebrew, and Greek thought, rested on the idea of domination by a male God, served by a male hierarchy. Woman was viewed with great fear and suspicion. The act of procreation within a legal marriage was considered the only justifiable sexual act; all else was sinful and labeled as lust.

In Judeo-Christian theology the naked female body came to be personified by Eve, the perversely bent rib of Adam, and Eve herself came to be used as a cipher for sin, sex, and death. In the societies of the early Christian West, "it was women's bodies, permanently implicated by Eve's sin, that symbolized the fact that humanity exists in a state of sinfulness and punishment."[1] Or, as stated in Ecclesiasticus, written by a Hebrew scribe of the early second century BCE: "From a woman was the beginning of sin; and because of her we all die" (25:24). Such myths are not exclusively Hebrew or Christian. The story of Pandora as retold by Hesiod (see chap. 4) is an example of how an earlier myth can be twisted out of its original form and recreated into a new myth, which, in turn, blames woman for all the ills of humankind. It is hardly surprising that a mythic creature like Baubo, who represented women's sexual power, would have had difficulty existing in a period permeated by such misogynous attitudes. But she was never completely eliminated. She took on new shapes, somehow retaining her basic attributes of sexual energy, transformation, and the balancing of opposites. Her Medusa mask was turned into the horrible gaping mouth of Hell or into a medieval image known as the Vagina Dentata. Her vulva, detached from its symbolic procreative function, was affixed to the devil and the devil's spawn. As the devil's whore she became the "great whore of Babylon" described so graphically in Revelation. And finally, in that most terrifying and ignominious period of the Inquisition in Europe, a time of intense persecution of women as witches, she became identified with witchcraft.

In medieval Western societies that defined woman as Eve, "Eve was simultaneously the mother of all human beings and the first sinner. Her naked body was an iconographical device that associated female nakedness with fecundity and evil, sexual desire and death. . . . Female bodies, from

FIGURE 10.1 *Gorgon-like figure with winged lions. From the cathedral at Piacenza, Italy. Twelfth-thirteenth century* CE.
(Andersen, 1977, fig. 26; Devereux, 1983, p. 185, fig. 31.)

the perspective of male fears and fantasies, are not only sinful and dangerous but quintessentially grotesque."[2]

The many grotesque female images found in Romanesque churches must be understood in this light; for the function of these strange female figures "was to identify, define, and thus to stabilize a feared and fantasized object."[3] Margaret Miles notes an added benefit: "Grotesque figuration contributes the bonus of laughter, permitting relief of tension; the simultaneously feared and desired object becomes comic."[4] An example of this sort of bizarre image can be seen in a statue placed in the cathedral of Piacenza, Italy (see fig. 10.1). This Romanesque "grotesquerie" squats in the posture of earlier Medusas, but the two winged lions by her side are

FIGURE 10.2 *Double-tailed mermaid over the main entrance at the Cathedral of Saint Michael, Lucca, Italy. Thirteenth century* CE. (Author's drawing from photographs by Betty Burkes and Paul Nossiter, 1989.)

portrayed as great pussycats, and her face has lost its mask-like aspect and much of its fierceness.

These early medieval female images were often combined in a playful manner with animals, even portrayed as part animal. The mermaid, one such popular combination, was possibly a dim memory of archaic water-snake goddesses, like Tiâmat or Danu (see fig. 10.2). Single- or double-tailed mermaids are frequently found motifs on many medieval religious structures. The cathedral of St. Michael at Lucca, Italy, built in the thirteenth century, contains a number of mermaid fantasies. On a central frieze directly over the main entrance, a decorative mermaid spreads her double tail in proud display of her genitals, while her sisters sport up and down ornately carved pillars of the four-tiered cathedral façade. A fiercer version of a double-tailed mermaid is found in Spain on a twelfth-

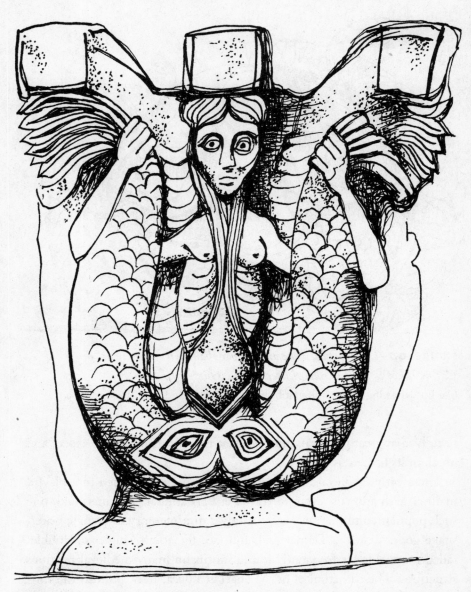

FIGURE 10.3 *A double-tailed Spanish mermaid. From a cloister capital at San Pedro de Galligans, Gerona, Spain. Twelfth century* CE. (Duby, 1981, fig. 7.)

century cloister capital at San Pedro de Galligans. This mermaid grasps her fish tails, which are equipped with fish eyes set just below the vulva (see fig. 10.3).

A curious echo of Baubo, known as La Potta di Modena, can still be seen in the cathedral at Modena, Italy. It dates from before the twelfth century and is a representation of a seated, grim-faced woman, with knees spread wide apart, naked except for shoes. Three pouch-like objects that hang over, or in place of, the vulva may be male genitals (see fig. 10.4). Much folklore has collected around this ambiguous androgynous Potta of Modena. In Italian street slang, *potta*, as a feminine noun, is still in use as a rude slang equivalent to the English "cunt." But *potta* also occurs in the masculine, as in the expression "essere il potta di Modena," meaning to boast. I am told by a friend from Modena that *potta* in current usage refers to a type of man known as extraordinary, or what we might call macho. She tells me that a surviving legend recalls how, long ago, a certain king of France, hearing of the magical potency of this legendary *Potta*, traveled from his land to the cathedral of Modena. On arrival, he placed himself squarely in front of La Potta and exposed himself before it—a gesture that local historians explain as an act of defiance or, possibly, boastful comparison.

In the ancient world, the androgyne was not an unusual concept. Bisexual images date from earliest antiquity, ample precedent for La Potta di Modena. In later medieval Christian times, the androgyne was firmly relegated to hell, where it proliferated, giving birth to all manner of devils with both male and female attributes. Woman by herself was seen as a dual image: As Virgin she was an unthreatening image, the impenetrable, the enclosed safe garden; but woman was also most significantly the whore. In medieval iconography the prostitute, the great whore of Babylon with whom the kings of earth had fornicated, came to epitomize "the penetrable body, the body shaped by lust, the permeable body that produces juices and smells."[5] The great whore was a popular image, taking over from Medusa as an image of dread and power.

A magnificent Apocalypse manuscript from northern Spain, created in 776 by Beatus, a monk at the monastery of Liebana, depicts the great whore of John's nightmares in all her splendor. As painted by Beatus she sits astride her seven-headed beast, whose tail ends in an extra horned

FIGURE 10.4 *La Potta di Modena. Modena Cathedral.*
(Salvini, 1956, fig. 224.)

head. She holds aloft the golden cup filled with her abominations. The great whore is clothed, her potent body hidden beneath a resplendent scarlet and purple gown. She is, truly, "mother of harlots and of the abominations of the earth" (see fig. 10.5). Just as Medusa's image persisted for centuries in the Hellenistic world, with her awesome mask constantly being revised, so this image of woman persisted as pollutant and as a symbol of sexual lust.

A curious "magic scroll" from Ethiopia redefines the same iconography (see fig. 10.6). Such scrolls, made under the influence of a living Hebraic-Christian theology, were still being created as late as the nineteenth century in the Ethiopian church. This scroll shows a holy hermit, Abba Samuel, riding his lion. In his left hand he holds a large cross, which he uses to exorcise a small hairy demon hovering above the lion's head. His other hand firmly grasps the lion's tail, while under the lion's belly squats a

FIGURE 10.5 *The Whore and the Beast. Based on a tenth-century facsimile of an eighth-century manuscript illumination.*
(Beati, 1962, p. 209R.)

small naked woman. Abba Samuel's gaze is fixed on the crouching woman. It may be that the scroll represents woman as whore tempting the holy hermit, or it can be read as the old apotropaic image of Baubo, protecting a holy man from the Evil Eye, or one could see this as Samuel, an image of church authority, trampling sin in the form of sinful woman, Baubo.

The figure of a squatting woman is repeated in the imagery of Western religious art throughout Europe. Sheilah-Na-Gig refers specifically to

FIGURE 10.6 *Ethiopian magic scroll. Early nineteenth century. Institute of Ethiopian Studies, Addis Ababa, Ethiopia.*
(Mercier, 1979, p. 72, pl. 17.)

naked female figures carved in stone and incorporated into many church buildings in Ireland and several in Wales and England. They date roughly from the twelfth to the sixteenth centuries. Once, there may have been hundreds of these carvings. We know that during the eighteenth and nineteenth centuries a great number were still in place on church walls and above doorways, but religious and social prudery has forced removal and destruction of most of them. In 1866 Thomas Wright published a volume in London entitled *The Worship of the Generative Powers During the Middle Ages in Western Europe* in which he listed and illustrated a few examples of Sheilahs he found in Ireland alone. Some of these Sheilahs had been dug up from the vicinity of ancient churches and are now housed in museums. Today, only a few remain as part of their original buildings.

Many variant spellings occur, including Sheilagh-Na-Gig, Sheela-Na-Gig, and Sheelagh-Na-Gig, among others. Margaret A. Murray, one of the first trained archaeologists to study these Sheilahs seriously, states simply that the name means "woman of the castle" and possibly nothing more than that.[6] But in her view, the Sheilahs should be regarded as divine, or at least as having divine attributes, because they were invariably found in Christian churches or, like most of the Irish examples, can be verified as coming originally from church structures. Barbara Walker says the name "meant something like 'vulva-woman!' *Gig* or *giggie* meant female genitals and may have been related to the Irish 'jig' from the French '*gigue*,' in pre-Christian times an orgiastic dance."[7] But the name may have a much older origin. In the Sumerian city of Erech, according to Merlin Stone, "The women of the temple were known as *nu-gig*, the pure or spotless."[8] Yet another theory is that "'shee' in Irish means half-spirit and half-human, and that Sheilahs were the children of Lilith."[9]

All the Sheilahs are female and naked, portrayed in a frontal *hocker* position, with hands either indicating the genitals or, more frequently, actually parting the labia. Breasts are sometimes minimal, often with flat chests and exposed ribs. Some of these sculptures are grimacing and have most unpleasant expressions; a few have skull-like death heads. They are indeed startling images, crude and mysterious. One of the most frequently reproduced Sheilahs is from the church of St. Mary and St. David in Kilpeck, Hereford, England, and is usually dated as 1140 (see fig. 10.7). In contrast to this Kelpeck Sheilah with her engaging grin, an Irish Sheilah,

FIGURE 10.7 *Sheilah-Na-Gig from Kilpeck Church, Herefordshire, England. Ca. 1140* CE.

(Devereux, 1983, title page; and Murray, 1934, pl. XII, #29.)

found in a church in County Cavon and now in the National Museum in Dublin, has a bestial, loathsome aspect. Her face has an open Gorgo-type mouth with tongue just visible. Her breasts are not indicated, only her bony ribs, while her hands hold a large prolapsed vulva (see fig. 10.8). To me, she seems to demand: "Don't dare turn away from me! I am sovereign! I am womb. I create Life and will repel Evil, even Death!"

Thomas Wright, writing in 1866, felt that the Sheilahs "were intended as protecting charms against the fascination of the evil eye."[10] Anne Ross, a Celtic authority writing in 1973, felt that the so-called Sheilah figures might have been portrayals of ancient Celtic goddesses, including Cail-lech, long remembered in the traditions and rituals of the Celtic peoples.

> Many of them have local names; and the goddess in her hideous and sexual form with her pronounced genital organs would be a highly apotropaic talisman; belief in the power of the exposed genitalia of either sex to avert evil powers is widespread. Once Christianity was established in Ireland, and elsewhere, the powers believed to be inherent in such pagan figures would be tapped, as it were, by the Church and used to keep malevolent forces away from the sacred dwellings, and from the tracks across dangerous country where many of them stood.[11]

Thus Ross sees the Celtic goddess as having a dual nature, appearing in her frightening, powerful, and highly sexed hag form and, alternatively, in her guise of womanly loveliness. She quotes from an Irish tale that describes a "many-shaped lady," who says, "I am the sovereignty of Erin. . . . As you have seen me loathsome, bestial, horrible at first and beautiful at last, so is the sovereignty."[12]

Questions about the Sheilahs remain. Were they, as Murray, Wright, and Ross contend, apotropaic remnants of pagan Celtic goddesses of creation and destruction? Why then did the Catholic Church continue to allow them to be displayed in conspicuous positions on sacred buildings? Why were they not eliminated with the church's usual efficiency?

Murray's own answer demands consideration. She wrote in 1934: "It is very evident that the appeal of the Baubo figures and of the Sheilah Na-Gig was to the sexual side of woman's nature, and in the legend of Baubo the attitude is definitely connected with pleasure and laughter. The religious connection is so strong, both among the heathen and the Christian,

FIGURE 10.8 *Sheilah-Na-Gig from County Cavan, Ireland.*
(Andersen, 1977, fig. 83; Murray, 1934. pl. xi, #25; Simpson, 1987, p. 109.)

as to suggest that some form of homo-sexuality was practiced by women as a religious rite."[13]

Murray also reports the following bit of folklore that she collected about one particular Sheilah statue found in a small Oxford church. She says that "all brides were made to look at the figure on their way to church for the wedding."[14] From this Murray builds a hypothesis that such figures might have been used to arouse or stimulate sexual desires of the brides. Murray conducted some inconclusive experiments among a few of her female colleagues and students, showing them Sheilah photographs. She claims that the sight of the images had a stimulating effect on her subjects, whereas the sight of male priapic figures produced only disgust or curiosity.

I do not share Murray's conviction that these vulva-displaying Sheilahs represent or were designed to stimulate women's overt sexual longings and hidden desires. The images are too stark, too brutal in their directness for this simple explanation. Rather, I agree with Ross that they relate to earlier Celtic goddesses in their dual aspects. The Sheilah with her Gorgon mouth, skeletal ribs, skull head, and accented vulva is both a death symbol and a regenerative image. She affirms that creation overcomes death. The wry grin of the Kilpeck figure echoes the grin on Baubo's face when she performed her routine before Demeter.

The few scholars, predominantly male, who collected these medieval church sculptures referred to them as female exhibitionistic figures. Viewed as immoral images that were curiously placed in churches, they combined moral warnings for vulnerable male and female souls. The Sheilahs were graphic warnings of the danger of female seductiveness that leads to hell. In a book recently published in England, they have been called "images of lust"![15]

Jorgen Andersen has traced the development of the Sheilah images from French Romanesque churches to their use in England and Ireland during the later Middle Ages. Commenting on the reason for these images' placement in churches, Andersen writes, "Devotion does not shrink away from showing the things that drag men down, grotesque shapes, frightening and ludicrous."[16] He sees "the Baubo as an interesting parallel to the Sheela, although not in any way directly connected with her"[17] and considers the Sheilahs demonic figures that yielded protection against demons by the frightening, "evil-averting influence of the vulva."[18] But Andersen also wisely observes, "One may learn from primitive art that to ward off evil and to promote fertility are functions which do not exclude each other, and this has a bearing on the function of Sheelas, who may be considered as mainly apotropaic, but occasionally lending themselves to fertility beliefs."[19]

Devereux, however, makes an interesting distinction between the Sheilahs of Ireland, Wales, and England, on the one hand, and similar grotesqueries and images of demonology found in French medieval churches, on the other. In his opinion, the French demons were personifications of creatures who tormented the damned rather than the damned themselves, who were condemned to the flames:

> One might say that these hideous representations of women [the Sheilahs] could be viewed as reminders to the faithful of the pious maxim that we are all brought into life between urine and excrement, and therefore the Sheilah images were created to disgust both men and women, who, starting with Eve, were the instigators of sin.[20]

In the late medieval period the rules of the game changed. Images that earlier had been understood as playful demons or timely reminders to the faithful of pious maxims now were seen in grim and deadly seriousness as personifications of the devil or as the devil's whores, as objects to be exterminated (see fig. 10.9). In Europe by the fifteenth century, the full weight of the organized misogyny of the Christian Church descended on Eve and her sisters. In 1484, Pope Innocent VIII published his first papal bull against witches. *Malleus Maleficarum,* an official document of the Inquisition that was written by two German monks and first published in 1486, was reprinted fourteen times before the year 1520. It remained an official Christian Church text for three centuries, the complete manual on how to investigate, interrogate, and execute witches. The *Maleficarum* states variously: "All witchcraft comes from carnal lust, which is in women insatiable . . . that she is more carnal than a man, as is clear from her many carnal abominations. . . . Wherefore for the sake of fulfilling their lusts they consort even with devils." The *Maleficarum* asserts that because all women "have slippery tongues, and are unable to conceal from their fellow women those things which by evil arts they know; and, since they are weak, they find an easy and secret manner of vindicating themselves by witchcraft. . . .

FIGURE 10.9 *A medieval witch. Detail from "The Witch's Sabbath," a wood engraving by Hans Baldung Grien.*
(Duerr, 1985, p. 48.)

Therefore, all women are potential witches, and "it is no wonder if the world now suffers through the malice of women."[21]

In this climate of fear and fury, the floodgates of gynocide in Europe were opened. Thousands of women and men suspected of witchcraft were put to death. The campaign of extermination led by the Inquisition was particularly ruthless in Germany, France, and England. The number of executions has been estimated "at an average of six hundred a year for certain German cities—or two a day, 'leaving out Sundays.'. . . At Toulouse, four hundred [women] were put to death in a day. In the Bishopric of Trier, in 1585, two villages were left with only one female inhabitant each. Many writers have estimated that the total number killed was in the millions. Women made up some 85 per cent of those executed—old women, young women and children."[22]

William Irwin Thompson addresses the effect of such attitudes:

When Woman's Power is taken from her, and when the old sisterhood of the matrilineal order is displaced, the power of women can no longer be direct and open, for direct military power is precisely the force which has displaced the feminine for the masculine order. The feminine compensation for this shift in the natural balance of things is a shift in sexual emphasis from fertility—that is, reproductive power—to erotic power. . . . What we now encounter in the male order of civilization is "sexiness," the erotic power of the beautiful woman to lure the powerful man to his own destruction.[23]

In such imbalance, the figure of Baubo inevitably lost its earlier significance. Her image became tarnished, and thus it is not surprising that she continued to be thought obscene, pornographic, and vulgar.

CHAPTER ELEVEN

During times of stress people become concerned about whether the energy vital to human life is being drained by energy inimical to life. During these times ancient metaphors for sexual identities become particularly salient. These metaphors determine which sex, if either, is blamed and which is held responsible for restoring order.

—Peggy Reeves Sanday[1]

The She and the He of It

An idealized vision of Attic Greece persists for us as a shimmering image of marble temples set under cerulean skies, of public spaces and public places adorned with white and gold statues of the Olympians. This stereotypic vision derives in large part from our museums of the past century, with their endless corridors and galleries lined with larger-than-life gods and goddesses, each discreetly draped and fig-leaved. In actuality, ancient Athens must have been a colorful city: There is considerable evidence that much of the municipal statuary was painted in brilliant colors in a manner that would seem garish to us today. We also know that two particular images representing male and female sexual power were conspicuous—Medusa and Hermes.

Baubo and her counterpart, Medusa, were dual embodiments of female sexual power, transformative symbols permitting the world to balance and perpetuate itself. In ancient Greece, Medusa was commonly seen in all her glory on temple pediments and public wall paintings, while brightly painted and carved images of the Gorgon's decapitated head appeared over doorways and were placed atop rooftops of private as well as public buildings. They were an accepted and important part of the Attic cityscape.

Although Baubo has already been examined in her various manifestations, Hermes is a new character and needs some explanation. Hermes and Baubo, a curious pair, rarely appeared together in legend and have not usually been linked by historians or scholars. I propose, however, to do just that, because in my opinion they share a number of unexpected similarities, the most obvious being their personification as sexual images—Baubo as vulva, Hermes as phallus. By juxtaposing one image against the other I hope to show that in the ancient world they were regarded as sacred symbols and not as pornography.

Hermes was a Greek deity of many aspects. He is best known to us in his role as messenger to Zeus, but in fifth-century Athens one of his most popular forms was that of a public phallic statue or *herm*. Herms were everywhere in the city—found at street corners, before the gates of dwellings, placed in front of temples, libraries, and gymnasiums, and much in evidence at the *agora*, or marketplace. These herms were four-cornered blocks of hewn stone, each topped with a sculpted head of Hermes, usually depicted as a dignified bearded god (see fig. 11.1). In the appropriate position on the front side of each stone block was a realistically carved erect (ithyphallic) phallus. We do not know if these herms were painted, but there is little doubt that, between the Medusas and the herms, "the she and the he of it" was highly visible throughout Athens.

At some point between 520 and 514 BCE, Hipparchus, ruler of Athens, decreed that hundreds of stone herms were to be set up as milestones, extending from the central altar in the agora out along the main road leading into the countryside. Hipparchus ordered these new statues as replacements for earlier piles of stones that had traditionally served as

FIGURE 11.1 *A garlanded herm statue. Detail drawn from an amphora now in the Museum of Fine Arts, Boston, item 68.163, L.T. Clay Gift.* (See also Boardman, 1985, fig. 364.)

boundary markers or cairns. *Herma* is the Greek word for a standing stone or pile of rocks. Hermes, known as "he of the stone heap," was divine protector of roads, crossroads, and journeys and of merchants and craftsmen and other travelers. Therefore it was appropriate for a ruler to install these new milestones stretching out from the city marketplace indicating to all who passed that Hermes protected and supported the trade and territorial claims of Hipparchus, the mighty sovereign of Athens.

Why were these erect phallus stones considered so potent? Were they descendants of the gigantic stone statues of winged phalli that once stood at the ancient sanctuary on Delos, a small Aegean island sacred to Apollo? Broken fragments of these monumental penises still rest on stone bases at Delos, mute testimony to the religious thought that sanctified human sexuality and reproduction. Were they fertility symbols, or were they, like the Gorgon's head, thought of as images bringing good luck or averting evil? Some scholars contend that the phallus, by its very nature, must have been a general image of fertility. Others insist that the phallus was simply an apotropaic amulet attached to Hermes, magician and god of the boundary stone.

Walter Burkert finds scant evidence for a fertility theory of herms. He argues that they were not commonly "set up in stables or folds, nor in the cornfields, and not necessarily in the bedroom. They stand in front of the house, in the market place, at crossroads, and at frontiers."[2] He reasons that the phallic stones represented "an action of display . . . a demonstration which transmits a message of potency in its double sense."[3] In other words, the herms became public apotropaic images, just as Medusa's contorted face (once associated with the vulva symbol of Baubo) evolved into symbols and signals projecting dual messages of fear and aversion or protection from forces of evil.

Where did these herms originate? Some claim that Hermes came from the wild and remote mountains of Arcadia, that his father was Zeus and his mother a nymph called Maia. According to one popular Greek legend, Maia gave birth to her son in a dark cave on the slopes of Mt. Kyllene, "where he [Hermes] was worshipped as an ancestor god . . . and at Kyllene in Elis his image consisted simply of a penis erectus."[4] He was an archaic Arcadian god of flocks, responsible for the fertility and well-being of sheep and goats. In this pastoral role he was popularly depicted not as a phallus but bearing a ram upon his shoulders or carrying a lamb.

Another theory of origin places Hermes north of Arcadia, on the islands of Lemnos, Imbros, and Samothrace, which lie at the gates of the Hellespont. This theory is documented by an ithyphallic image of Hermes found on a coin from Imbros and in an account by Herodotus. According to Herodotus, these islands were settled by the Pelasgians or "people of the sea," who came to dwell among the Athenians, teaching them the sacred rites and mysteries of Samothrace. It seemed clear to Herodotus that the Pelasgians also taught the Athenians to carve ithyphallic statues of Hermes and that the Athenians were the first of all Greeks to create these images.[5]

The Arcadian version of Hermes' origins became the dominant Greek legend and has shaped our image of Hermes. Rather than an erect phallus, his persona has come down to us as an ebullient and brilliant charmer. That is how he is portrayed in the seventh-century *Hymn to Hermes*, which appears in the same collection of thirty-three pseudo-Homeric hymns that includes the *Hymn to Demeter*.[6] Hermes is presented as a trickster, magician of spells and words, musician, inventor, thief, and servant. In this long poem detailing the adventures of Hermes, there is absolutely no mention of an ithyphallic herm.

Both Hermes and Baubo were often seen in the role of Olympian servants. Although the son of Zeus, Hermes was a divine servant because he was born to a mortal nymph, and he was constantly at the beck and call of his master-father. He performed with perfection "all that was expected of a diligent servant—skill in lighting the fire, splitting kindling wood, roasting and carving meat, pouring wine."[7] He was chief steward and messenger of Zeus. In the *Hymn to Demeter*, Iambe (Baubo) was a mortal servant, first to Metaneira and then to Demeter. As the quintessential nurse-servant "always knowing her duties," she remained ever faithful to the goddess and Persephone. The position of Baubo among the immortals is ambiguous. The chief evidence for her immortal status comes from two inscriptions found at Paros and Naxos (see chap. 3), where her name was inscribed next to Demeter, Persephone, and Zeus.

Evidence from literary, inscriptive, and iconographic sources makes clear that Iambe/Baubo and Hermes, whether mortal or semi-divine, shared the ability to move betwixt and between, to glide in and out of situations and places. They were able to cross between heaven, earth, and the underworld. They both were given the epithet "*chthonius*" (*chthonos* meaning earth or underworld). Hermes Chthonius, chief messenger of Zeus, was renowned as an important psychopomp or escort of souls and was at ease traveling in the skies or down in Hades. At the command of Zeus, Hermes Chthonius escorted Persephone up from the realm of the dead to rejoin her mother back on earth. And herein lies another of the curious intersections that link Hermes and Baubo. According to later Orphic elaborations of the myth, It was Baubo Chthonius who acted as the guide for Persephone on her subsequent yearly journeys between earth and underworld.[8]

Baubo and Hermes were skillful connection makers. Neither hesitated to make use of magic or jokes or trickery to achieve desired ends; and although they shared a keen delight in pranks and a comic sort of eroticism, neither was ever known to use humor in destructive ways. They were consistently friendly and helpful to women and to men, and their humor was often allied to their knowledge of magic. This is easiest to see in the many legends concerning Hermes, for he was usually portrayed well equipped with winged sandals, magic hat, and his famous magic wand, the caduceus. The golden caduceus of Hermes was made in the shape of a staff with two serpents entwined around a central rod. Homer describes it as a fair and golden staff that Hermes used whenever he chose to lull the eyes of men and again to waken them from his magic spell, for Hermes was famous for his word magic. He was called "The Whisperer" or "Master of the Magic formulae which bind."[9] He was able to use his wand or words wherever "magic is needed to overcome the distrust of the stranger and break down the taboos on social intercourse."[10]

Baubo, too, used jokes, even obscenities, as magic formulas to overcome the resistance of the goddess and to assuage the grief and anger of Demeter. Baubo, too, was a "whisperer of words" and used them with unerring psychological skill and insight, just as she used her gesture of *ana-suromai*. Iambe/Baubo, the servant-nurse, had magic knowledge and was thoroughly versed in the use of herbs when she mixed the special drink or *kykeon* for Demeter. It must not be forgotten that in many ancient cultures a nurse traditionally used herbal and other "magic" lore, as illustrated in

Hymn to Demeter where the goddess, disguised as an old nurse, attempted by magic acts of fire to make the infant prince Demophoön immortal. Baubo also understood the magic boundaries of taboos when she performed her astonishing feat of staging the lively antics of the baby Iacchus on her bare belly. In the accounts given by Clement and Hesychius, Baubo is without doubt a taboo smasher.

Yet for all their magic skills and abilities, Hermes and Baubo remained realists. Both were able to assess and accept difficult situations and then move on. They used whatever means were at hand, whether magic or trickery, to search out acceptable ways of change. Brown calls Hermes a "culture hero . . . giver of good things . . . who defended his people against the aggressions of strangers."[11] These words apply equally to Baubo; both figures, in their respective ways, were consistently benevolent and always attempted to promote the welfare of human beings.

It is not surprising that images of such force persisted, that Hermes and Baubo, with different shapes and names, were amalgamated into Roman myth. Baubo's imagery merged with the goddess Isis and her rituals. Hermes, the messenger god, became synthesized into the Roman god Mercury, swift as quicksilver, who retained the caduceus of Hermes, his magic wand. In Rome, neither the ancient winged phallus on Delos nor the Athenian herm was forgotten but rather was transmuted into a very popular image of a small flying penis-bird. This object may have had erotic connotations but more than likely retained traces of earlier sacred power.

A fragment of a stone carving has been found in Gallo-Roman ruins in Nîmes, France, dating from the first or second century CE (see fig. 11.2). This stone carving is an odd amalgam of Hermes and Baubo symbols. It represents a bird, either a hawk or a phoenix, with outstretched wings. Two bells hang on ribbons from the creature's neck. Its tail is a penis, and its strong clawed feet cover a clutch of four eggs. The eggs are vulvas. When an engraving of this penis-bird from Nimes was first published in 1825, it was regarded as an amusing oddity, representing a rude form of priapic worship from southern Gaul.[12] Linking it with the legends and iconography of Baubo and Hermes, however, makes possible another interpretation. It becomes yet another link to the unbroken chain of manifestations of superhuman sexual energy, female and male, which once were understood to have sacred power.

FIGURE 11.2 *A phallus-bird nesting over vulva eggs. Stone carving from Roman-Gallo ruins, Nîmes, France. First–second century* CE. (Wright, 1957, pl. III.)

An even stranger companion image of "the she and the he of it" was found in England, dating many centuries later than the bird-penis of Nîmes. A stone carving that has survived from the fifteenth century (perhaps earlier) can still be seen on a church tower at Whittlesford, Cambridgeshire (see fig. 11.3). This stone slab is set high on the tower over an archway. Baubo is easily identified on the left, squatting in her familiar hocker position. Stretching across to her is an ithyphallic figure whose pursed lips attempt a curiously gentle kiss. Margaret Murray, who first published a photograph of this carving in a 1934 article, identified the couple as a "Sheila-na-gig with a man-animal,"[13] in which there is a faint indication of a tail waving over the male rump. Just as I do not dismiss the herms of Hipparchus or the bird-penis of Nîmes as erotic oddities, I do not dismiss this English carving as simply an amusing bit of mediaeval drollery. It is

FIGURE 11.3 *Sheilah-Na-Gig kissed by a "man-animal." Carving from a church tower, Whittlesford, Cambridgeshire, England. Fifteenth century* CE. (Murray, 1934, pl. XII, #32.)

paradoxical that it was part of a building for Christian worship and was never removed. This surely indicates some residue of sacred importance, some tenuous tie with the sacred sexual attributes of Baubo and Hermes.

Judeo-Christian institutions were fairly successful in Europe in their efforts to sweep away and bury pagan sexual sacred iconography. In the climate of Far Eastern culture, however, these beliefs and their symbology were never interrupted, and in fact they continue to flourish. Nowhere is this more apparent than in India, particularly in Hindu Tantric art and ritual. Tantric imagery leaves no doubt of the religious significance of these powerful symbols (see fig. 11.4).

Tantra derives from Indian Buddhist traditions that became dominant in the fifth century. Mircea Eliade observes that "the conception of this cosmic Force personified in a Great Goddess was not invented by Tantrism. Pre-Aryan India, and the popular India in which it survives, have known the worship of the Great Mother since neolithic times, whatever its forms, names and myths may have been. . . . Tantrism strove to rediscover

FIGURE 11.4 *The Divine Yoni. A Tantric wood carving from southern India. Nineteenth century* CE.

(Rawson, 1973, p. 17, fig. 7.)

in the body and the psyche themselves the cosmic power personified in the Great Goddess."[14]

In Tantric ritual the greatest energy is understood as sexual and the sexual organs represent cosmic powers, especially those of the all-powerful Shiva. The lingam (phallus), worshipped as the symbol of Shiva's creative power, is the strength that made him the greatest of all gods, the god of cosmic fertility. The yoni (vulva) was also worshipped as the symbol of his consort, Shakti, who has many aspects. As Devi or Durga, she is the Tantric goddess of terror, and is then a consort of Shiva in his personification as god of destruction and regeneration. Sometimes she is known as the fierce Kali, or Dirga the black Kali; but as Parvati or Uma she is also a gentle, mild-mannered goddess, worshipped in that guise as the Great Mother. She is the unity of all of the goddess aspects. She is always the yoni representing feminine force and principle.

Tantrism visualizes male and female sexual energy as the motive force that sustains the universe. Thus yoni and lingam are frequently combined in one image, one body. This image, the he/she, or androgyne, is a symbol of great antiquity. In Tantric ritual it is used as a metaphor for the reconciliation of opposites. Virginia Woolf understood this reconciliation of opposites when she wrote, "It is fatal to be a man or woman pure and simple; one must be woman-manly or man-womanly."[15]

Hindu worship designated Ardhanarîsvara as the one deity who combined female and male attributes, the deity who signified psychic totality. Figure 11.5 is a detail redrawn from a seventeenth-century bronze amulet of this deity. The Devi Goddess is depicted with upraised arms in the act of blessing the holy. She is incorporated with the ancient male symbol of the bull, who holds the triangular yoni image within his great horns. This amulet, made in Himachal Pradesh, India, over three hundred years ago, is a fitting correlative of Virginia Woolf's words. It is an image of a particular way of thinking, a way of being, to borrow Ajitcoomar Mookerjee's words, in which

> women and men are not at war, but through their collective uniqueness realize the feminine fullness of the universe. They are the images on earth of the unitary cosmic principle, and in *imbalance* [emphasis added], they disturb the macrocosmic equilibrium. The two must be one in male-female relationships, in order, as Vivekananda put it, to "restore the essential balance in the world between the masculine and feminine energies and qualities. The bird of the spirit of humanity cannot fly with one wing."[16]

Again, we return to Baubo. This is language she would have understood and applauded.

FIGURE 11.5 *The Devi, Goddess Ardhanarîsvara, who combines the female and male. Bronze amulet. India, seventeenth century* CE. (Mookerjee, 1988, p. 27.)

This book concludes with two appendices offering contrasting mythic characterizations of the Baubo archetype. The first is a synopsis, including translated portions, of the Attic *Hymn to Demeter*, one of my starting points. The second appendix contains several myths gathered from other cultures, ancient and modern, to provide a sense of the ubiquity and metamorphic nature of Baubo's spirit across cultural space and time.

Innumerable other examples of such myths wait to be collected, myths telling of female transformative power. New images of archaic great goddesses are constantly being unearthed, and the challenging task remains of correlating these images with the ancient legends. Not only should they be collected; they must be reevaluated. All of us, women and men, are just beginning to grasp the significance of both iconography and myth, beginning to understand that they represent a history of a large part of the life force of this planet. These myths may help us to find that in the final and crucial years of this century, the key word may be planetary *balance*.

Baubo/Iambe as energizer of Demeter, comforting the sorrowing goddess; Baubo/Isis as nurturer standing before the gods of Egypt; the ancient forerunners of Baubo, revealed in carvings and glyphs; and the Tantric yoni—each of these figures in its own way represents the connection between woman's transformative power and the creative powers of the earth. For in order to maintain the balance of the earth, Baubo and her sisters have not hesitated to exhibit their female power before the face of furious goddesses or even before armies. The halting, comical, "dutiful" Baubo is triumphant as a timeless and culturally unbounded expression of woman's sexual energy.

Persephone Abducted by Hades[1]

Homeric Hymn to Demeter (*Synopsis*)

The opening lines of the *Hymn to Demeter* state the theme of this poem, written during the seventh century BCE:

> I sing of lovely-haired Demeter, the awesome Goddess
> and of her slender-ankled daughter, who was abducted by Hades,
> with the connivance of Zeus, the loud-thunderer who sees all.[2]

The scene of the abduction and rape of Persephone is vividly described. The young girl is seen in a meadow with her companions, as they gather violets, irises, narcissus, crocuses, and roses. Zeus, the schemer, however, had placed one particularly beautiful hyacinth as a lure for his child. Thus, when Persephone bends over to pick this flower, "The wide-pathed earth in the Nysian plain / opened up and out sprang upon her / Lord Polydegmon, the all-receiver, Hades on his immortal horses" (16–18). Hades seizes the girl and, forcing her into his chariot, bears her away to his underworld kingdom. Although she shrieks and fills the air with lamentations, "Only tender-hearted and wise Hecate, the daughter of Persaeus / with the bright headband, who was inside her cave, heard the girl's cries" (24–25).

Eventually the girl's shrill cries, reverberating from the underworld, reach the ears of Demeter.

> With her precious hands
> she tore the veil from her divine hair, and tossing
> the dark cloak from her shoulders, she sped like a bird
> over dry lands and seas—ever searching for her child. (40–43)

The mighty goddess searches all over the earth for nine days. She begs for news of her daughter from all the gods, but not one comes to her aid. Hecate finally, out of pity for her grief, helps Demeter in her search. When she learns the truth, the furious goddess

> abandoned the assembly of gods on high Olympus
> and came down to the cities and rich fields of men,
> where she concealed her divine form for a long while. (92–94)

Demeter continues her anguished search and comes at last to the town of Eleusis. She sinks heart-sick by the roadside on a stone at the Maiden Well, where the women of the place are accustomed to draw water. No one can recognize her because she disguises herself so that "she resembled a worn-out old woman, born long ago, / who was cut off from child-bearing and from the gifts of garland-loving Aphrodite" (101–2).

At the well, Demeter is found by four young girls, daughters of the ruler of Eleusis, who had come to draw water. They approach the old wanderer with due courtesy and suggest that she return with them to their parents' house, where they assure her she will be welcome and well cared for. Demeter, giving her name as Doso, responds with a fanciful tale to account for her presence by the well. She tells of leaving Crete, of her subsequent capture by pirates, and of her long wandering. She ends this recital by saying to the girls,

> I might nurse a new-born child, carefully cradling it in my arms,
> or I might oversee a household where I would spread the coverings
> on the master's bed in that innermost part of the well-built chamber;
> or I might instruct the serving women in their tasks. (141–44)

The narrative continues as the four girls speed home and tell their mother, Metaneira, about the stranger. They obtain permission and return to persuade the disconsolate goddess to come to their father's great hall. On arrival, they approach the inner courtyard, where Metaneira is sitting with her cherished only son, Demophoön, upon her lap. As the veiled Demeter crosses the threshold on slender feet, "Reverence, awe, and pale fear seized hold of Metaneira. / She rose from her chair and urged the stranger be seated" (190–91). Demeter refuses and remains standing in silence with downcast eyes.

It is at this point in the hymn that Iambe, a comical but faithful servant of the household, appears and places a wooden stool next to the stranger-guest, first throwing a soft-silvery fleece over the seat. Demeter accepts, but continues to hold her veil before her face. "For a long time, silently, she sat there with sorrowing heart. / Responding neither by word or gesture, never smiling / and without tasting either meat or drink" (198–200).

Iambe then steps forward to confront the disconsolate goddess in the grip of her black mood.

> Iambe, always knowing her duties,
> with much jesting and joking caused the holy lady
> to smile and to laugh and to have a gracious heart,
> and afterwards as well she pleased her moods. (202–5)

The narrative makes it clear that Iambe's jokes and quips are important to Demeter, so endearing her to the goddess (laughing amid her grief), that she keeps Iambe with her as a servant, or perhaps as one of her priestesses.

The hymn continues with Demeter's stubborn refusal of the cup of sweet wine offered by Metaneira, requesting instead a special nourishing drink made of barley meal, water, and pennyroyal (mint). This potion, called *kykeon*, subsequently became one of the more important elements in a kind of communion service in the Eleusinian Mysteries. Refreshed by the *kykeon*, Demeter listens politely to Metaneira's proposal that she serve her and King Keleos by becoming wet nurse to Demophoön, the newborn, long-awaited son of this ruling family. Demeter gladly accepts this role, responding,

> And hail to you, also, lady, may the gods grant you good fortune.
> I will gladly take charge of this child just as you command me,
> and will certainly nurse him. (225–27)

Having thus spoken, "Demeter received the baby in her immortal arms and clasped him / to her fragrant bosom, while Metaneira rejoiced in her heart" (231–32).

After this episode during which Demeter eventually reveals her true identity, the hymn returns to its central theme—the rape and disappearance of Persephone and the great anger of the goddess. Demeter, seated now in her newly-built temple, grieves with ever-renewed intensity over the loss of her child. In her fury she causes a dreadful and withering agricultural year,

> the most terrible year for men on the all-nourishing earth.
> The seed was not able to sprout from the ground,
> for the golden-crowned goddess kept it hidden. In vain the oxen
> pulled the many curved plows over the fields,
> and in vain much white barley was scattered upon the land.
> She would then have utterly destroyed the race of mortal men
> by a cruel famine and would even have deprived those dwelling
> on Olympus of their sumptuous sacrifices and honors. (305–12)

These conditions force Zeus to act. The succession of gods he sends to assuage Demeter comes bearing gifts, but no one can calm her. She rejects all their endearments. "Never, she said, would she set foot on fragrant Olympus / nor allow the fruits to spring forth from the ground on earth, / until with her own eyes, she had seen her fair-faced daughter" (331–33).

Having failed to find a successful scheme to remedy the situation, Zeus—the loud-thunderer—capitulates. Finally, he chooses Hermes, the fleet-footed messenger god, as his emissary, sending him down into the hidden places of the world with orders that Hades, Zeus's brother, must release Persephone at once. Hermes succeeds in securing an agreement with Hades to return Persephone to her mother. The reluctant Hades, however, slips a single pomegranate seed into his young wife's mouth just before she mounts the chariot for their journey up to earth. This nourishment from the underworld begins its lasting effect as Hermes takes charge of the chariot and delivers Persephone to her mother.

When Demeter, waiting in her temple, sees the chariot approach, "she ran to her daughter, / just as a maenad rushes down some densely wooded mountain slope" (385–86). This meeting is related in great detail, as mother and daughter share their grief and joy and tell each other their tales of separation and wandering. But the intense happiness of their reunion is muted as Demeter learns from Persephone of the pomegranate seed her daughter inadvertently swallowed before beginning her journey from the underworld. For, in consequence of this act, Persephone must spend a third of the year in the dark and hidden places of the earth, the remaining time with her mother:

> When the earth blooms in spring with all sweet-smelling flowers,
> then from the misty gloom of the underworld you will rise again,
> a great wonder for gods, a great wonder for mortal men. (401–3)

The concluding sections of the hymn tell of Demeter's reconciliation with the community of Olympians, of how, with Persephone seated again beside her, the goddess relented, permitting a return to the natural balance of things,

> so that the whole wide earth
> was heavy with green leaves and flowers. (471–72)

The close of this marvelous poem is concerned with those sacred rites and rituals that Demeter taught the Athenian people. The verses establish the legendary origins of the ceremonies at the festivals in honor of Demeter, which were repeated at Eleusis each year for many centuries.

APPENDIX 2

Three Gorgon-Baubos—The Menacers and Protectors[1]

A Selection of Myths Reflecting the Spirit of Baubo

The myths presented in this appendix from a wide range of cultures are strikingly similar in structure. In each, a deity withdraws in anger and humiliation because of the misdeeds of another; usually the offended one is a deity of earth or sun or weather. Thus, forces vital to the regeneration of all planetary life are withdrawn, and the survival of humankind is threatened. The insulted one (in most cases, a goddess) eventually is placated and cajoled into cooperation with the basic needs of mortals by a ribald female figure. This second figure, by the bold expression of her sexuality and by a combination of humor and dance or some other pointed physical gesture, restores balance and harmony to the world.

The narratives repeat the theme of women's sexual energy and power and contain reworkings of this basic theme, echoing Baubo's action before Demeter. I believe they are representative of an array of ancient and not-so-ancient stories that imply in various ways the same story. For "a myth is not a linear code, but a polyphonic fugue,"[2] and "in the richness and complexity of the myth, no earlier level is abandoned; all are included. Each succeeding level of culture surrounds and incorporates the previous one; thus a myth about the evolution of culture becomes itself a performance of the evolution of culture."[3]

Myths that come from cultures temporally or geographically distant from our own are often accepted with amused tolerance as curiosities. But they merit closer study, especially when they constitute a long-obscured part of our cultural heritage that is now re-emerging. For in many myths the motif of female power is at the heart of the matter, and frequently in these myths it is the laughter of a woman that plays a crucial part in restoring balance and harmony to the beleaguered earth.

In the myths presented here, often the laughter is between women, using private jokes intended only for each other. Sometimes the laughter is between sexes, but the jokes neither insult nor denigrate. The laughter serves rather to comfort, to help the insulted one regain wholeness and power.

The first myths are a Hittite tale and a Sumerian version, both written down around 2000 BCE. The Hittite myth tells of the disappearance of Inara, a daughter of the great storm god. In another version of this same tale it is Telipinu, the youngest son of the storm god, who vanished after a bitter quarrel. Both deities are "survivors of a native pre-Hittite pantheon which formed the basis of the second millennium religious system,"[4] when even older matrilineal traditions of goddess worship were still vital.

The third and fourth myths are ancient Egyptian tales concerning aspects of the goddess Hathor. They were found in scrolls in tombs or inscribed on temple walls. In both of these myths, Hathor acts as mediator in the interminable conflicts of the gods, skillfully using a gesture identical to Baubo's *ana-suromai*—and, again, her laughter.

Another myth comes from pre-modern Japan. It describes the tribulations of the sun goddess Amaterasu and her difficulties with her wild brother, Susanowo, the storm god. This tale recounts how the goddess was aided and abetted by Uzume, a lesser goddess of dance and mirth and how together they managed to restore the earth to harmony and balance.

And finally, from the Philippines comes a myth in the making, telling of an action that Kalinga tribal women initiated only a few years ago in a mountainous region of Luzon. Here is a myth, not inscribed on stone or clay or on papyrus, but rather recounted in an interview and preserved on a videotape made in 1984. These Philippine women in their dedicated efforts for their people and their land reached deep down into sources of mythical behavior to create their own myth.

INARA AND TELIPINU
A Hittite and Sumerian Tale

The Hittites flourished during the middle of the second millenium BCE on the high central plateau of Anatolia (Turkey). They gradually conquered all of Anatolia, parts of Syria, and northern Mesopotamia. Their warrior empire came to an end by 1200 BCE. In 1906, German archaeologists uncovered great archives of clay tablets from the Hittite capital city of Hattusas (now called Boghazkoy). Because the Hittites had adopted the Babylonian cuneiform script, scholars had little difficulty in deciphering the tablets. From this store of clay tablets emerged a chronology of Hittite invasions and conquests, as well as many of their legends, myths, and rituals.

The Hittites were Indo-European, related to the Greek, Roman, and Indic peoples. Thus it is possible that many of their myths could have filtered down into latter-day Aegean myths. One of these Hittite myths describes the disappearance of a goddess or a storm god and bears many resemblances to the Demeter story. The most complete tablet series tells how Telipinu, a young storm god, vanished taking with him the whole of life.

Telipinu is sought for, eventually found, brought back, and appeased by rituals. There are variant sets of this Telipinu tale on clay tablets; and on one fragment, Inara, the daughter of the old storm god, is now the heroine in place of Telipinu. Another fragment tells the same disappearance story with Hannahanna, the Mother Goddess, in a leading role. The substitution of a god for a goddess was commonplace among records of primordial deities; and frequently the same myths and the same basic myth motifs were applied to both sexes. This is especially true in Hittite and Egyptian myths.

The Telipinu version is the most accessible to us because of excellent translations of the surviving text tablets. Telipinu, youngest son of the storm god, was a provider of rain and the supreme god over all of western Asia. In this fragment, he has had a fight with his wife, Ashmunikal. He gets so angry that "he put his right shoe on his left foot . . . and left." He goes off to the steppe country and there gets lost, carrying away all growth, everything good.[5]

The tablet reads:

> Fog seized the windows, smoke seized the house:
> In the fireplace the logs were "oppressed" [smoldering],
> On the pedestal the gods were "oppressed,"
> in the fold the sheep were "oppressed,"
> in the corral the cows were "oppressed":
> The ewe refused its lamb, the cow refused its calf.
>
> .   .   .   .
>
> Barley and emmer-wheat no longer grow,
> cattle, sheep and humans no longer became pregnant,
> and even those who are pregnant do not give birth.
> The mountains dried up, the trees dried up
> (so that) the shoots did not come (forth).
> The meadows dried up, the springs dried up.

The analog with the Demeter myth is quite clear so far, and, as in the Greek story, when the gods as well as humankind begin to suffer, the holy ones are forced to take action.

The great sun god intervenes at this point and summons all one thousand lesser gods to a feast. After appropriate feasting and drinking, the gods decide to go in search of the missing Telipinu. They ask the keen-eyed Eagle to help them, but even he fails. The Eagle reports back to the assembled gods:

> The high mountains I searched,
> the deep valleys I searched,
> the dark blue waves I searched,
> but I did not find him, the Storm God of Heaven!

The gods meet together and decide to ask for help from the grandfather of the storm god, telling him how the seed has perished and how everything has dried up. The old man gives them little satisfaction, placing all the blame on the gods themselves. He says: "No one sinned, but you *alone* sinned!" and then he threatens to kill them all.

So the gods turn to Hannahanna, the ancient grandmother, the Great One, who asks:

> "Why do you come?"
> [The distraught gods answer:]
> "The Storm God became enraged,
> (so) everything dried up and the seed perished.
> Now my father says to me:
> 'It is your fault!
> I shall investigate the matter and kill you!' "
> [The wise and patient Hannahanna replies with these words:]
> "Fear not!
> If it is your fault I shall put it straight,
> and if it is not your fault I shall (also) put it straight.
> Go, search for the Storm God."

Agreeing to take charge of the search, Hannahanna summons the Bee to her, and although the gods grumble that the Bee is too weak and its wings too frail, Hannahanna gives the Bee exact instructions, where and how to search. Following the Grandmother's directions, the Bee flies off and searches everywhere. She finally discovers Telipinu asleep under a tree in a hidden grove, and she stings him on the hands and feet, just as she had been instructed. Telipinu, awakened by the bee stings, becomes furious. He then wreaks even greater havoc on man and beast and on the whole world. Powerful and magic rituals are required to overcome this fury of the god. Here, this particular tablet series breaks off, and the story must be reconstructed with fragments that fit from other tablets.

Another version of the myth is even more fragmentary. Here Inara, the daughter of the old storm god disappears. As in the more complete version, the Eagle searches for the goddess but returns without finding her. And again, the venerable Hannahanna is summoned and commands the Bee to take part in the search. The Bee finds Inara and wakens her with bee stings on hands and feet. Only then, with the return of the goddess and after long and proper rituals, does the earth regain its fertility.

Whether the central role of disappearance is given to Telipinu or Inara, the basic theme is the fury of a fertility deity, who is capable of destroying life in all its forms. Both versions repeat the importance of magic rituals known and practiced by women, which can restore cosmic stability and well-being.

Yet another Hittite goddess appears in some versions of this tale. Kamrupsepa, a goddess of healing and magic, sometimes resolves the conflict. When Inara (or Telipinu) returns, fuming and furious and in pain from the bee stings, Kamrupsepa calms and soothes the offended deity with appropriate magic rites. Her rituals may well have included the use of honey, for in many parts of the ancient world the bee was a sacred and important symbol for the potency of nature. Honey was both valued as a food and used in healing potions. When mixed with "wise blood" (menstrual fluid), it was considered the universal elixir of life.

A fragment from one Hittite tablet gives some credence to the idea that the disappearance of the deity (whether Telipinu or Inara) was not simply a retreat into the forest, but rather a trip into the underworld. The tablet reads:

> The doorkeeper has opened the seven doors. . . .
> Down in the dark earth there stand bronze cauldrons,
> their lids are of Abaru metal, their handles of iron.[6]

The fragment then ends with the return of Telipinu to his house.

The similarities in structure between these Hittite myths and the Demeter/Baubo story is evident: the insult, the anger, the withdrawal or disappearance to the underworld, the effect on the world of that withdrawal, and the consolation. There is, however, one significant difference in tone: the Hittite myth contains no laughter. There are no jokes or jests, none of those impudent dancing gestures of Baubo. If any humor existed, it is not evident in the clay fragments that have been found. The Hittite tale is somber in tone, even grim.

A Sumerian poem called *The Descent of Inanna*, also dating back to 2000 BCE, has similarities to both the *Hymn to Demeter* and the Hittite tale of Inara. The Sumerian goddess Inanna, full of anger, also caused the green of the earth to wither. She also threatened the earth with barrenness and humankind with extinction. Inanna was a "*life*-goddess, a goddess of the process of living and goddess who caused the procreation of others, but who did not herself procreate."[7] She was not a mother, but rather a fertility-goddess. Some of the Sumerian poems that have been transcribed from clay tablets include lyric and graphic celebrations of Inanna, her body, and her sexuality as sacred entities. "The goddess's body and her sexuality were subjects for celebration, not for reticence and shame."[8]

Demeter has her servant, Iambe/Baubo, while Inanna has her faithful servant or sukkal, Ninshubur. In the *Descent of Inanna*, when the goddess vanishes for many days underground, Ninshubur takes her place at the gate of the underworld and waits for her mistress. She has donned soiled sackcloth, the garments of mourning, and she crouches on the ground, waiting. When the *galla* (demons) emerge, escorting the goddess back to earth, they offer to release Inanna in exchange for Ninshubur. Inanna answers them:

> No! Ninshubur is my constant support.
> She is my *sukkal* who gives me wise advice.
> She is my warrior who fights by my side.
> She did not forget my words.
>
> She set up a lament for me by the ruins.
> She beat the drum for me at the assembly places.
> She circled the houses of the gods.
> She tore at her eyes, at her mouth, at her thighs.
> She dressed herself in a single garment like a beggar.

Alone, she set out for Nippur and the temple of Enlil.
She went to Ur and the temple of Nanna.
She went to Eridu and the temple of Enki.
Because of her, my life was saved.
I will never give Ninshubur to you.[9]

Ninshubur and Iambe/Baubo stand similarly beside their respective mistresses. The succinct words in the Homeric *Hymn to Demeter* (lines 202–4) remind us that trusty Iambe stayed for some time in the goddess's service, that she continued with jokes and jests to cause the holy lady to smile and to laugh and thus made her heart cheerful.

TWO EGYPTIAN MYTHS OF HATHOR

Two recorded myths from Egypt echo the tale of Demeter and Baubo. They differ in many details, but both use the basic pattern of woman's sexual power or energy as a balancing influence in a situation where male disharmony or aggression has run rampant.

In the first of these Egyptian myths, Hathor (or Sekmet, as she is called in her fierce lion aspect) restores equilibrium to the land. This version of an ancient story has been recovered and reassembled from various inscriptions carved into the stone walls of burial chambers in the royal pyramids of the fifth and sixth dynasties. Hermann Junker, a German archaeologist, gathered the fragmentary texts in 1910. They are now known collectively as the "Pyramid Texts" and are dated circa 2300 BCE.

A few facts about Egyptian religion may be helpful in understanding these stories. Egyptian gods and goddesses have a confusing way of assuming multiple names and of shifting from one gender to another, making it difficult to keep track of them.

For the Egyptians, mythology was not a collection of texts, but a language. This is fundamental. It explains why the doings of the gods could be altered, be expanded and even reappear with other protagonists without apparent inconsistency. But myths do not have to be consistent. They belong to a way of thinking in which consistency in the logical sense is irrelevant. The myth was a way, and before the emergence of lay philosophy with the Greeks, the only way, to express ideas about the cosmos or the needs of the human soul. This is why Egyptian mythology is so simple, so absurd and sometimes so profound. It is dream, metaphysics and poetry, all at once.[10]

Egyptian gods and goddesses were complex characters with many different aspects that varied in time and place over the immensely long period of Nilotic culture. Egyptian deities were commonly addressed by multiple names, names that changed depending on the district or city where they were worshipped.

Thus Rê, the most important god, called "the complete one," was also known as Atum, or Ra-Atum, which means "all or nothing." Rê was said to have come from the primal waters and to have created himself, first by masturbation, then by spitting. One of the surviving texts—called the "Coffin Texts" because they were found in tombs written on cloth or papyrus wrapped around royal mummies—reads:

> I am Atum, the creator of the Eldest Gods,
> I am he who gave birth to Shu,
> I am that great He/She,
> I am he who did what seemed good to him. . . .[11]

Hathor, like Rê, was a complex deity of many names and aspects. She represented a synthesis of all notions concerning cosmogenesis and was known as "the great one of many names." Hathor was revered in her benevolent aspect as Amaunet, Lady of the Sky and the Primeval Ocean. She was frequently depicted in her cow form as Hathor-Meheturt, as a great cow who gave birth to the solar system. Her iconograph was a cow swimming in the cosmic ocean and carrying a solar disk between her horns. As Hathor, lady of the sacred sycamore tree, she gave suck to the pharaohs and was worshipped as a daughter of Rê. As Hathor-Taueret, she was portrayed as a hippopotamus, standing on her hind legs, with distended belly and hanging breasts; and Taueret was always shown wearing the solar disk, horns, and head-plumes of Hathor. She was goddess of childbirth and patron of marriage and nourishment. The rituals of Hathor, in later dynastic times, merged with those of the benevolent cat goddess, Bast, who presided over mirth, gaiety, and music, over drink and dance. It was Hathor as Bast who was celebrated in festivals at Bubastis described by Herodotus (see chap. 3).

Hathor could also assume the aspect of Sekmet, a warrior goddess, also known as Sekmet the Lion-Headed. Hathor/Sekmet at such times incarnated the fierce and awesome power of Rê or the Eye of Rê. Sekmet was then known as the Golden One, a symbol of light. It is in this warlike role of both Sekmet and the Eye of Rê that Hathor appears in the first of our Egyptian myths.

This Pyramid Text opens abruptly after Sekmet quarrels with her father, Rê. The reasons for the quarrel are not given on the extant inscriptions. In any case, Sekmet, in a rage, intends to destroy the universe and then depart for the deserts of Nubia. She "threatened to wash the very earth back into the primordial sea and to return to Her ancient form of the great serpent."[12] The goddess's departure plunges the land into gloom and sterility, for Sekmet-Hathor, as a wild lion, prowled the desert, a terror to humans and animals, and death took over. The text goes on to tell how she chews flesh, drinks blood, and puffs fire from her eyes and nostrils. Sekmet becomes the Golden One's aspect of death and destruction, and the bleak Nubian desert becomes a symbol of the underworld.

As time goes by, Rê comes to regret this quarrel with his own daughter. He misses her company and, perhaps, regrets losing her ferocious skills as a defender. He feels vulnerable to enemies and increasingly aware of his isolation, "for he began to grow old, his bones became silver, his flesh gold and his hair [as] real lapis lazuli."[13] He is a stiff old man, and lonely. He decides to end his quarrel with Sekmet-Hathor. So he sends two of his sons, the gods Thoth and Shu, disguised as monkeys, (or lions, according to another text), to search for Sekmet. He gives them precise and urgent instructions for persuading her to return. Whether lions or monkeys, after a long and arduous search, they find the lion-faced goddess camped upon a high rock in the desert.

They tell the goddess piteous tales of the suffering that her prolonged absence has caused her people, which eventually touches her compassionate Hathor nature. After much persuasion, Sekmet agrees to give up her wild and savage desert life and return with the gods to the civilized world of the Nile delta.

A number of colorful versions tell of the return of Hathor/Sekmet. She was said to have been accompanied by a huge retinue of baboons, Nubian musicians, dancers, and comic figures. This triumphal procession moved from city to city along the Nile with noise and gaiety and festivals given in her honor all along the route. It was said that as she traveled northward away from the desert, the goddess changed; her lion-faced Sekmet aspect disappeared and she became transformed into the charming, pleasure-seeking cat-faced Bast. The tale ends, as does the *Hymn to Demeter*, in peace, with Sekmet/Hathor/Bast restoring fertility and balance to the land and people of the Nile.

The second Egyptian Hathor myth was written down a thousand years later, in 1160 BCE. This papyrus, now in the British Museum, may be a version of a much earlier popular story. Certainly this episode, sometimes referred to as "The Ritual Baring of Hathor," is part of a longer irreverent and ribald tale called *The Great Contending*. The version that we have, known as the "Beatty Papyrus," consists of one strip of papyrus, 16 feet long and 8 inches wide. The story, although not illustrated, is written in an elegant black and red cursive script.

In contrast to the fierce lion-headed Sekmet aspect of Hathor in the Pyramid Text story, Hathor appears throughout *The Great Contending* in her role as the gracious and compassionate Lady of the Sycamore. The story opens with details of an involved lawsuit and a bitter quarrel between the gods that has dragged on for more than eighty years. The crucial issue concerns the legal succession to the throne of Rê: whether the god Seth or the god Horus should assume kingship of Egypt.

In *The Great Contending*, the assembly of thirty gods is heartily sick of the continual disturbance that the two contestants have created throughout the universe. The papyrus graphically describes their bloody struggle. During one confrontation, Horus wrenches off the testicles of Seth, who, in turn, tears out the left eye of Horus. Finally, the two contenders are persuaded by Thoth, a god of order, to submit their dispute to the council of gods for arbitration. The gods listen carefully but can reach no decision. Letters are then dispatched summoning the opinions of yet more gods and goddesses, and the council reconvenes to try to resolve the question.

The thirty gods reassemble in the great hall, but they continue to shout taunts and recriminations at each other. At this point in the proceedings, Baba, a lesser monkey god with red ears and a red bottom, long known as a mischief-maker and confuser, taunts great Rê by shouting at him, "Thy shrine is empty!"[14] thus implying that no one worships any longer or pays any attention to the aged god Rê. Rê is so "aggrieved at this taunt which had been spoken to him, he laid himself down upon his back, and his heart was very sore." Then the company goes outside and turns on Baba, saying:

> Get thee forth, this crime that thou hast done is extremely great. And they went to their tents. And the great god passed a day lying upon his back in his arbour, and his heart was very sore, and he was alone.
>
> After a long space, Hathor, the lady of the southern sycomore [*sic*] came and entered before her father, the Master of the Universe, and she uncovered her nakedness in his face. And the great god laughed at her.

Thereupon he rises up and resumes his place, sitting down with the thirty gods, and the meeting reconvenes. Horus speaks, then Seth has his turn. The members of the council once again have their say, and eventually the Great Contending is resolved. Still more trials take place, but legality triumphs finally over brute force. Horus is selected, and the white crown of Egypt is set upon his head.

My interest in this tale lies not in the clash between two ancient political systems, nor the rivalry for power, nor the struggle over inheritance of kingship, but rather in Hathor's role in the episode and her oddly inappropriate ritual unveiling. In the Beatty papyrus the passage reads: "She uncovered her nakedness in his face. And the great god laughed at her." What was that all about? Why did Rê laugh?

Gardiner in his note on this passage says: " 'Nakedness' in my translation represents a grosser word in the Egyptian text."[15] This brings us full circle back to Baubo, her *koilia*, and her gesture of *ana-suromai* before Demeter. Once again, we are dealing with a potent female divinity, representing the forces of fertility and nourishment, who appears at crucial moments of strife and confrontation and who, by the baring of the reproductive parts of her body, says: "Look here! Let's get this affair back in balance! Enough of this nonsense!" It is repetition of the advice of Hannahanna, the Hittite grandmother: "If it is your fault I shall put it in order, and if it is not your fault I shall put it straight." We are dealing with a similar sense of cosmic equilibrium.

A short but crucial word in Gardiner's translation raises a significant issue. In Gardiner's version, "Rê laughs *at* Hathor." Rundle Clark translates the same passage: "She bared her private parts before him, so that he was forced to laugh thereat."[16] The difference may be subtle, but to me it seems important. According to Clark, Rê is laughing not *at* Hathor but *with* her; "thereat" refers to her joke. The difference is vital. In my reading, this is no simple scene of seduction. No erotic arousal is implicit in Hathor's stance. The lady of the southern sycamore is not attempting to titillate her father; she is arousing his humor, his laughter, in order to return Rê to a saner view of the problem, to help him regain balance.

Notice another important point in these lines. If the bisexual nature of Rê is accepted and if it is understood that Rê represented "the great he/she of the primal waters of the universe," the Egyptians of that time might well have thought of the ritual baring as something done by Hathor before the *mother* aspect rather than the father aspect of Rê. In this reading, Hathor, like Baubo in front of Demeter, was helping a female parent figure to a more objective view of the bitter controversy. She was revealing their shared center, the vulva of procreation, indicating the sacred symbol of their return to origins, the place of renewal and regeneration. In this reading, the laughter of Rê in her bisexual form was laughter provoked by Hathor's gesture, a healing and regenerative sign.

These two Egyptian myths show Hathor as a sacred woman, who, freed from anger, brings her strength to the earth and allows the world to green again and fructify. It is in this manner that she is depicted on a wall painting from the tomb of Ramses VI, 1150 BCE. Hathor is painted standing before Rê. She is naked, wearing a broad necklace but without her ceremonial headdress. Placed alongside her body are crocodiles, scarab beetles, a bull, a man, and the figure of the ram-headed god holding the sphere of the cosmos. By her feet, two arms are raised in the gesture of Ka, "a symbol of the transmission of life power from gods to men."[17] She holds a solar disk in one hand and in the other a small falcon-headed figure. This is the quintessential symbol of the female force as balancer.

THE MYTH OF AMATERASU

It seems reasonable enough to suppose that Hittite, Egyptian, and Aegean cultures should have similar mythic tales, but when basically the same tale appears in Japan, that requires a shift in thinking. A well-known Japanese myth about Amaterasu, the sun goddess, is surprisingly close in both structure and detail to the Greek Baubo-Demeter story.[18] It was recorded first in the *Kojiki* ("Records of Ancient Matters") and again in the *Nihongi* ("Chronicles of Japan"). These versions written down about 710 CE were probably derived from much earlier oral versions.

This Japanese myth recounts the outrageous behavior of Susanowo, the storm god, who was the brother of the sun goddess and known as "the impetuous male." He quarreled continually with his sister, Amaterasu, "the heavenly shining one," who again and again made excuses for her brother's "impetuous misdeeds" and forgave him.

But one day Susanowo goes too far. He not only rampages in his sister's newly planted heavenly rice fields, trampling in the irrigation ditches, but he voids his excrement inside Amaterasu's sacred temple, just before her celebration of the First Born. The patient goddess is prepared to forgive even this. Then Susanowo seizes and kills a piebald colt of Heaven, breaks a hole through the roof tiles of his sister's weaving hall, and flings the bloody carcass down among the sacred silk looms.

This terrible scene causes a great disturbance, and in the commotion one of the weaving priestesses pricks herself with her shuttle and falls dead. Other versions say that it was Amaterasu herself who was grievously wounded in her vagina by the flying shuttle. But all versions agree that the "heavenly shining one" then flees in fear and anger, seeking refuge in the Cave of Heaven. Once inside, safely away from her brother and his brutal pranks, the goddess Amaterasu fastens the rock doorway and refuses to come out.

The world is plunged into darkness. There is no day, only night. Nothing can grow on earth, making life impossible. This causes great consternation among the Eight Hundred Gods, who gather before the cave where Amaterasu is hiding by the Riverbed of Heaven, trying to lure her out. They chant sacred rituals; they collect birds of the Eternal Land (roosters), who sing constantly to each other; they decorate the Sahaki trees that stand before the cave with long strings of precious jewels and soft blue and white cotton banners; and on a branch nearest the cave entrance they hang a large gleaming object, a newly created invention—a round mirror made of polished bronze. Yet Amaterasu resists all their enticements and refuses to come out. The world stays dark and infertile.

Finally, a goddess of dance and mirth is summoned to come and aid the gods. She is called Ama-no-Uzume of the many names; she was also known as "the terrible female of heaven" or "Uzume-Ota-Fuku" (she of the big breasts). She is famous for her own special Kagura, a laughter-producing obscene dance.

Ama-no-Uzume arrives and arrays herself with bamboo leaves and other plants. She then climbs upon a large upturned tub placed by the cave entrance. Uzume begins her dance, drumming her feet on the hollow tub, and as the ecstasy seizes her she opens her kimono and removes her undergarments. The Eight Hundred Gods roar with laughter at this performance, and the cocks of the Eternal Land join in the hullabaloo with their crowing.

The noise is so great that even the sun goddess hidden away in her cave hears it. Curious to see what is happening, she peers through a peephole in the doorway and sees her own reflection in the strange new bronze mirror hanging just outside. Fascinated by her own reflection, she comes a little way out of the cave, whereupon one of the gods swiftly stretches a rope behind her, preventing the goddess from stepping back into the dark cave.

As soon as Amaterasu appears, the sun's rays once again shine brightly and the normal alternation of day and night resumes. The gods decide this time to punish Susanowo themselves. They make him pay a heavy fine, and then they pluck out his beard and mustache and banish him from Heaven.

The parallels between Amaterasu and Demeter are quite obvious, as are those between Ama-no-Uzume and Baubo. The two supportive figures employ the *ana-suromai* gesture in the same way, and in both cases the anger of the deity is deflected and assuaged. Laughter is employed similarly. The roles of the rampaging males are also alike—Susanowo with his "impetuous misdeeds" and Zeus and his brother Hades with their rapes and aggressions and sulks. And in structure, both myths feature a nurturing goddess who withdraws in anger, causing darkness and infertility on earth. The most important parallel is the use of a woman's laughter or laughter-provoking gesture to bring the world back into balance.

A MYTH IN THE MAKING FROM THE PHILIPPINES

We are inclined to think of myths as stories from the distant past, but there are also myths in progress. This example of a myth in the making comes from the Philippines and deals with the assertion of female primacy, which is really what Baubo is all about, and with women's understanding of their connection to the survival of life, of the fertility of our earth.

This is not a written myth but rather an oral one that describes a mythic action occurring not long ago. Mariflor Parpan, an anthropologist from the University of Manila, offered the story as part of her description of an action that had recently taken place between the northern mountain peoples, the Kalinga, and lowland industrialists and bankers attempting to construct a series of four hydroelectric dams in northern Luzon, in the heart of the Kalinga's ancestral land. This project would have meant "the tragic displacement of a self-determining people, the genocide, or death of a people, their becoming paupers through wholesale displacement from their ancestral lands, from the primeval forests and rice terraces which their forefathers had created for them and made beautiful for the past thousand years."[19]

Parpan spoke on the subject of the wholesale dislocation of peoples by multi-business interests. She dwelt in particular on displacement, development, and impoverishment in her native land. She related how a vast hydroelectric project had been planned in the land of the Kalinga peoples:

> The dam would have put an area under water from the tip of one mountain to the tip of another mountain; the land of fifteen thousand families or one hundred thousand individuals.
>
> In numerous appeals and confrontations with government and electric company authorities, the Kalinga elders spoke again and again with great dignity and passion. They pleaded for "the land which is sacred and beloved, from whose womb spring our Kalinga lives." The electric

company officials answered these entreaties with contempt, saying that the Kalingas had no documents, no titles, to prove that they actually owned the lands they claimed. The elders replied, saying: "You speak of owning the land and you taunt us asking for proof of ownership. Such arrogance to speak of owning that which owns you! How can you own that which will outlive you? Only the race owns the land, for only the race lives forever.

Kalinga petitions and delegations to the lowland officials all failed, as did Kalinga legal actions. It seemed that, as in other areas of the Philippines, this series of hydroelectric dams could not be stopped.

It was at this point that the brave women of the Kalingas decided on a direct-action confrontation. According to Parpan:

It was an act of courage, sui generis, one of its kind, unheard of anywhere before. It was like this: When the engineering team to survey the mountain for the hydroelectrification project came, they were also escorted by almost a battalion-strong of soldiers, who went without as much as a by-your-leave. They started poking into the ground and in the process some boulders and sepulchers cracked and people were very outraged, because, among the Kalingas, as among most communities, ancestors are revered and their resting places are sacred places.

The survey operations continued, and the women decided that they would have to do something.

One day, they made flanking formations. They were dressed only in their native wraparound skirts, the Kahin, which is hand woven of a very heavy cotton. Among the Kalinga women when you are married then you usually wear only your Kahin, because that means you can breastfeed your baby more easily.

Clad only with this skirt around their waists, and armed with nothing except a few garden tools, the women made their way toward their garden patches. At a signal, they removed their skirts. They undressed—right before this group of men! And then, they used the heavy skirts to thrash at the men, and lash at them, and pin them to the ground. Some even wound the Kahins around the necks of the men.

Then very quietly, but very efficiently, almost as if it had been programmed, they removed all the survey implements and the guns, the weapons of the soldiers, who by this time, were too dazed and too embarrassed to do anything. And as well, they removed the men's clothes right down to their socks.

The women then took all the men's clothes and implements and weapons, some to the forest, some to the river; and the men had to hide in the bushes until dark, because they dared not go out in public without a stitch on. The helicopter had to come the next day to retrieve the implements. And the men stealthily stole into their own homes only after it was dark.

This act was really very clever. It manifested how profoundly the women understood lowland values [of the soldiers], as well as the values of their own highland men. You see, we have a cultural taboo—not to lay eyes or hands on women. It would be so unmanly, and it would be dishonorable. So they knew that their men would be disarmed immediately if they were in front of women who were naked. That is why the women removed their skirts. The men [soldiers] could not possibly hustle or tussle with them. What honor would there be in it? Fighting with a woman when you have no possibility of victory with her, much less a naked woman?

For the women also knew that to reach the nearest military and police outpost would require that the men would have to display their naked bodies, and that the men would never do, to go there without a stitch on. So the women could go back to their homes and be very sure that there would be no possibility of any military backup. The men waited in the bushes until dark, and by then, the women had gone innocently back to their homes.

According to Parpan, the Kalinga women took enormous risks by this direct-action confrontation. "They risked their own lives and their honor by showing themselves naked to strange men. And they also committed their *own* men to death, for their men would be duty bound to come to their aid [if the soldiers had attacked]. By this unprecedented action, the Kalinga women were saying: 'We resist! We oppose this act that would kill us as a people!' " In this case, their courage was rewarded, and, so far, a dam has not been constructed in the land of the Kalinga.

This *ana-suromai*-type of action by a phalanx of determined Philippine women constituted a formidable mass of concentrated sexual power and a reversal of conventional female behavior. It is not surprising that the men could not stand up to such a force. Yet there are other historical and mythical examples of large groups of women presenting themselves naked or raising their gowns before an invading male force in order to protect their lands.

In *The Bravery of Women*, Plutarch (46–120 CE) recounts an incident that occurred during a war between the Medes and the Persians. In a certain battle, the Persians, turned tail and fled before the strong advancing Median forces. Then the fleeing Persian warriors were blocked by their own Persian women, who derided them as cowards; and the women proceeded to lift their gowns before their own men. The Persians, in utter humiliation, turned and faced the enemy and finally defeated the invaders. Plutarch claimed that after this, whenever the king of Persia had reason to enter this city, he commanded that each Persian woman be given a golden coin.[20]

In the same volume Plutarch tells of the Greek hero Bellerophon, who rode his magic winged horse, Pegasus. Bellerophon had come to the aid of the Lycian people, but he was subsequently insulted by one of their leaders. In anger over this unjust treatment, Bellerophon waded out into the sea and prayed to Poseidon to render the Lycian land sterile and useless. Having made this prayer to the sea god, he returned to the shore just as wave after wave began to inundate the land. The men pleaded with Bellerophon as the sea threatened to cover the plain, but he was unable to stop the advancing waves. At this point, the Lycian women came forward. They waded out to meet the Greek hero, and they pulled their gowns up from their bodies, facing Bellerophon. In shame, he retreated back to the sea. It is told that as he retreated and as the crowd of women advanced in their gesture of *ana-suromai*, the waves also retreated and the Lycian land was saved.[21]

Another myth telling of the potency of collective female sexual energy comes from a very early Gaelic legend about Cú Chulainn. As a very young lad, Cú Chulainn had decided to do battle against his own countrymen. He could not be dissuaded from this disastrous plan. But then his path was blocked by a large contingent of women. Their female leader, Scandlach, stood before him with one hundred and fifty women:

and they all exposed their nakedness
and their boldness to him.
The boy lowered his gaze away from them
and laid his face
against the chariot,
so that he might not see the nakedness
nor the boldness of the women.[22]

In the context of such myths and historic memories, the Kalinga women's *ana-suromai* does not seem so strange and removed, as if it were a singular and bizarre act of a people utterly disconnected from our culture's familiar and predicating ways of thinking. Because the history of the Kalinga's threatened culture has yet to play out, we cannot yet identify the events of Mariflor Parpan's narration as something of true mythic importance. In fact, we will never be able to do that; only the Kalinga can establish their own defining myths. But should the Kalinga survive, should the threat of submersion beneath stagnant waters recede, we can easily imagine these events becoming central to how the Kalinga view themselves and their women. Like Baubo's actions before Demeter, or like even more ancient icons celebrating the nurturing power of women's sexuality, the ultimate result of the Kalinga women's act will be a blessing to the earth.

NOTES

BCE, "before the common era," is used in place of B.C., "before Christ," to divide time in a manner inclusive of both Christians and non-Christians. Likewise, CE, "common era," is used instead of A.D., anno domini, "in the year of the Lord."

PREFACE

1. Peggy Reeves Sanday, *Female Power and Male Dominance: On the Origins of Sexual Inequality* (New York: Cambridge University Press, 1981), 181.

CHAPTER I. UNCOVERING THE RUBBLE

1. From Robin Morgan, "The Network of the Imaginary Mother," in *Upstairs in the Garden: Poems Selected and New, 1968–1988* (New York: Norton, 1990), 69 (by permission of Edite Kroll Literary Agency).

2. Jane Ellen Harrison, *Prolegomena to the Study of Greek Religion* (1903; reprint, London: Merlin Press, 1980), 569.

3. Harrison, *Prolegomena*, 569.

4. Psellus in Harrison, *Prolegomena*, 568, trans. W. M. L.

5. Maurice Olender, "Baubo," s.v., *Encyclopedia of Religions*, ed. Mircea Eliade et al. (New York: Macmillan, 1987).

6. Maurice Olender, "Aspects de Baubô: Textes et contextes antiques," *Revue de l'histoire des religions* 202 (1985): 6. "Baubô: Nourrice de Deméter; signifie aussi cavité (koilia), comme chez Empédocle," trans. W. M. L. A shortened translated version of this article appears in *Before Sexuality: The Construction of Erotic Experience in the Ancient Greek World*, ed. David M. Halperin, John J. Winkler, and Froma I. Zeitlin (Princeton, N.J.: Princeton University Press, 1990). In my research I have relied on the original.

7. Olender, "Aspects," 7, trans. W. M. L.

8. Olender, "Aspects," 28, trans. W. M. L.

9. "Peasants in some parts of Europe are reported to believe that the moon menstruates and that she is 'sickening' during the period of waning, while the red rain or

heavenly blood, which old folklore asserts often falls from the skies, is 'moon-blood.'"
Esther M. Harding, *Women's Mysteries* (New York: Pantheon, 1955), 55.

10. William Irwin Thompson, *The Time Falling Bodies Take to Light: Mythology, Sexuality, and the Origins of Culture* (New York: St. Martin's, 1981), 109.

11. Marija Gimbutas, *The Goddesses and Gods of Old Europe* (Berkeley: University of California Press, 1982), 17. Gimbutas uses "Old Europe" to designate the collective identity and achievement of the different cultural groups in southeastern Europe, circa 7000–3500 BCE.

12. Olender, "Aspects," 30, trans. W. M. L.

13. Ronald Stroud and Nancy Bookidis, *Demeter and Persephone in Ancient Corinth* (Princeton, N.J.: American School of Classical Studies at Athens, 1987), 6.

14. Adrienne Rich, *On Lies, Secrets and Silence: Selected Prose, 1966–1978* (New York: Norton, 1979), 35.

15. Clarissa Pinkola Estés, *Women Who Run with the Wolves: Myths and Stories of the Wild Woman Archetype* (New York: Ballantine, 1992), 335.

CHAPTER 2. SAGE IAMBE AND RAUCOUS BAUBO

1. Ll. 202–5. All translations from this poem are by W. M. L. I have followed the Greek text of the *Hymn to Demeter* in *Hesiod, The Homeric Hymns, and Homerica*, ed. Hugh G. Evelyn-White (1914; reprint, Cambridge, Mass.: Harvard University Press, 1964).

2. Paul Friedrich, *The Meaning of Aphrodite* (Chicago: University of Chicago Press, 1978), 172.

3. Karl Kerenyi, *The Gods of the Greeks* (London: Thames and Hudson, 1951), 242.

4. Bella Debrida, "Drawing from Mythology in Women's Quest for Selfhood," in *The Politics of Women's Spirituality*, ed. Charlene Spretnak (New York: Doubleday, 1982), 145.

5. Maurice Olender, "Aspects de Baubô: Textes et contextes antiques," *Revue de l'histoire des religions* 202 (1985): 13, 14, trans. W. M. L.

6. Charles Picard, "L'Épisode de Baubô dans les Mystères d'Éleusis," *Revue de l'histoire des religions* 95 (1927): 229.

7. Olender, "Aspects," 21, trans. W. M. L.

8. Olender, "Aspects," 46, trans., W. M. L.

9. Ibid.

10. Nicholas J. Richardson, ed., *The Homeric Hymn to Demeter* (London: Oxford University Press, 1974), 216.

11. This ceremony is quoted from Georgios Megas and is included in Allaire Chander Brumfield, *The Attic Festivals of Demeter and Their Relation to the Agricultural Year* (Salem, N.H.: Ayer, 1981), 125.

12. *Hymn to Demeter*, ll. 450, 469.

CHAPTER 3. BAUBO VERIFIED

1. From Margaret Atwood, "A Red Shirt," in *Two-Headed Poems* (New York: Oxford University Press, 1978), 102 (by permission of the author).

2. Maurice Olender, "Aspects de Baubô: Textes et contextes antiques," *Revue de l'histoire des religions* 202 (1985): 15.

3. Olender, "Aspects," 15. Also see Charles Picard, "L'Épisode de Baubô dans les Mystères d'Éleusis," *Revue de l'histoire des religions* 95 (1927): 231.

4. Olender, "Aspects," 44. Olender cites Henri Jeanmaire, *Dionysos: Histoire du culte de Bacchus* (Paris, 1970), 197–98.

5. Olender, "Aspects," 39, trans. W. M. L.

6. Herodas, a third-century Alexandrian, wrote a series of amusing sketches entitled *Mimiambi*. In Mime 6 he describes two Alexandrian women visiting, gossiping, and comparing notes on the virtues of a particular dildo or baubon. The local cobbler had made it for one of the ladies from a very soft crimson leather.

7. Lawrence Durdin-Robertson, *The Goddesses of Chaldea, Syria and Egypt* (Enniscorthy, Eire: Cesara, 1975), 8.

8. Durdin-Robertson, *Goddesses*, 123.

9. Miriam Robbins Dexter, *Whence the Goddesses: A Source Book* (New York: Pergamon, 1990), 29.

10. Margaret A. Murray, "Female Fertility Figures," *Journal of the Royal Anthropological Institute of Great Britain and Ireland* 64 (1934): 95.

11. Herodotus, *Histories*, book 2, section 60, trans. W. M. L., based on the Greek text of *Herodotus*, ed. A. D. Godley (Cambridge, Mass.: Harvard University Press, 1920), 1: 346.

12. *Didorus of Sicily*, trans. C. H. Oldfather (New York: G. P. Putnam, 1933), 1.85.3.

CHAPTER 4. FESTIVAL SACRAMENT, SACRED LAUGHTER

1. Ll. 118–23. These and the following lines translated by W. M. L., based on the Greek text established by A. W. Mair in *Callimachus, Lycopphron, Aratus*, ed. and

trans. A. W. Mair and G. R. Mair (1921; reprint, Cambridge, Mass.: Harvard University Press, 1977), 135.

2. Walter Burkert, *Greek Religion*, trans. John Raffan (Cambridge, Mass.: Harvard University Press, 1985), 19.

3. Aristophanes, *The Frogs*, trans. David Barrett (New York: Penguin, 1964), 171.

4. *Hymn to Demeter* in *Hesiod, The Homeric Hymns, and Homerica*, ed. Hugh G. Evelyn-White (1914; reprint, Cambridge, Mass.: Harvard University Press, 1964), p. 322, ll. 478–79, trans. W. M. L.

5. George Mylonas, *Eleusis and the Eleusinian Mysteries* (Princeton, N.J.: Princeton University Press, 1972), 228–29.

6. Clement of Alexandria, *Protrepticos* (*Exhortation to the Greeks*), chap. 2, 17P.-18P., trans. W. M. L., based on the Greek text of G. W. Butterworth, ed., *The Exhortation to the Greeks*, in *Clement of Alexandria* (New York: G. P. Putnam, 1919), 42.

7. *Herodotus*, ed. A. D. Godley (Cambridge, Mass.: Harvard University Press, 1920), book 2, section 171, 1: 485.

8. Burkert, *Greek Religion*, 104–5.

9. Karl Kerenyi, *Zeus and Hera: Archetypal Image of Father, Husband, and Wife*, trans. Christopher Holme (Princeton, N.J.: Princeton University Press, 1975), 157.

10. Kerenyi, *Zeus and Hera*, 159.

11. Burkert, *Greek Religion*, 245.

12. Betty de Shong Meador, "The Thesmophoria: A Women's Ritual," *Psychological Perspectives* 17, no. 1 (1986): 40–41.

13. Bruce Lincoln, *Emerging from the Chrysalis: Studies in Rituals of Women's Initiation* (Cambridge, Mass.: Harvard University Press, 1981), 85.

14. William Irwin Thompson, *Evil and World Order* (New York: Harper and Row, 1976), 56.

15. Hesiod, *Works and Days,* in *Hesiod, The Homeric Poems, and Homerica*, trans. Hugh G. Evelyn-White (1914; reprint, Cambridge, Mass.: Harvard University Press, 1964), p. 7, ll. 57–58.

16. Eva C. Keuls, *The Reign of the Phallus: Sexual Politics in Ancient Athens* (New York: Harper and Row, 1985), 1.

17. Sarah B. Pomeroy, *Goddesses, Whores, Wives and Slaves* (New York: Schocken, 1975). Pomeroy is an excellent source for this information.

18. Jane E. Harrison, *Themis: A Study of the Social Origins of Greek Religion*, in *Epilegomena . . . and Themis . . .* (New Hyde Park, N.Y.: University Books, 1962), 230.

19. Keuls, *Reign of the Phallus*, 301.

20. Keuls, *Reign of the Phallus*, 350.

21. Mary R. Lefkowitz and Maureen B. Fant, eds., *Women's Life in Greece and Rome* (Baltimore: The Johns Hopkins University Press, 1982), 113.

22. Ruth Padel, "Model for Possession by Greek Daemons in Images of Women in Antiquity," in *Images of Women in Antiquity*, ed. Averil Cameron and Amélie Kuhrt (Detroit: Wayne State University Press, 1983), 7–8.

CHAPTER 5. BAUBO AND THE SCHOLARS

1. William Irwin Thompson, *The Time Falling Bodies Take to Light: Mythology, Sexuality, and the Origins of Culture* (New York: St. Martin's, 1981), 250.

2. William K. C. Guthrie, *Orpheus and Greek Religion: A Study of the Orphic Movement* (1952; reprint, New York: Norton, 1966), 135.

3. Charles Picard, "L'Épisode de Baubô dans les Mystères d'Éleusis," *Revue de l'histoire des religions* 95 (1927): 222.

4. Walter Burkert, *Greek Religion*, trans. John Raffan (Cambridge, Mass.: Harvard University Press, 1985), 104–5.

5. Manfred Lurker, *Dictionary of Gods and Goddesses, Devils and Demons*, trans. G. L. Campbell (New York: Routledge and Kegan Paul, 1987), 57.

6. Margaret A. Murray, "Female Fertility Figures," *Journal of the Royal Anthropological Institute of Great Britain and Ireland* 64 (1934): 95.

7. Nor Hall, *The Moon and the Virgin: Reflections on the Archetypal Feminine* (New York: Harper and Row, 1980), 45.

8. Friedrich Nietzsche, *Nietzsche Contra Wagner*, in *The Portable Nietzsche*, ed. and trans. Walter Kaufmann (New York: Viking, 1954), 683.

9. Johann Wolfgang von Goethe, "On Morphology," in *Goethe's Botanical Writings*, trans. Bertha Mueller (Honolulu: University of Hawaii Press, 1952), 109.

10. George Devereux, *Baubo, la vulve mythique* (Paris: Jean-Cyrille Godefroy, 1983), 52.

11. Clarissa Pinkola Estés, *Women Who Run with the Wolves: Myths and Stories of the Wild Woman Archetype* (New York: Ballantine, 1992), 336.

12. Jane Ellen Harrison, *Prolegomena to the Study of Greek Religion* (1903; reprint, London: Merlin Press, 1980), 534.

13. Murray, "Female Fertility Figures," 99.

14. Picard, "L'Épisode de Baubô," 236, trans. W. M. L.

15. Picard, "L'Épisode de Baubô," 238.

16. Maurice Olender, "Aspects de Baubô: Textes et contextes antiques," *Revue de l'histoire des religions* 202 (1985): 24, trans. W. M. L.

17. Olender, "Aspects," 26, trans. W. M. L.

18. George Mylonas, *Eleusis and the Eleusinian Mysteries* (Princeton, N.J.: Princeton University Press, 1972), 293.

19. Mylonas, *Eleusis*, 293.

20. Mylonas, *Eleusis*, 297–98.

21. Mylonas, *Eleusis*, 305.

22. Mylonas, *Eleusis*, 292 n. 8.

23. Walter Burkert, *Greek Religion*, trans. John Raffan (Cambridge, Mass.: Harvard University Press, 1985), 288.

24. Burkert, *Greek Religion*, 244.

25. Karl Kerenyi, *The Gods of the Greeks* (London: Thames and Hudson, 1951), 244.

26. Karl Kerenyi, *Eleusis: Archetypal Image of Mother and Daughter*, trans. Ralph Manheim (Princeton, N.J.: Princeton University Press, 1967), 40.

27. Kerenyi, *Gods of The Greeks*, 244.

28. Carl G. Jung and Karl Kerenyi, *Essays on a Science of Mythology: The Myth of the Divine Child and the Mysteries of Eleusis* (Princeton, N.J.: Princeton University Press, 1949), 159.

29. Jung and Kerenyi, *Essays*, 160.

30. Bruce Lincoln, *Emerging from the Chrysalis: Studies in Rituals of Women's Initiation* (Cambridge, Mass.: Harvard University Press, 1981), 72.

31. Lincoln, *Emerging*, 73.

32. Lincoln, *Emerging*, 80.

33. Lincoln, *Emerging*, 80–81.

34. Devereux, *Baubo*, 52, 101.

CHAPTER 6. THE IMAGE DEFINED

1. Muriel Rukeyser, "Painters," in *The Collected Poems of Muriel Rukeyser* (New York: McGraw-Hill, 1978), 543 (by permission of William Rukeyser).

2. Phillip Rawson, "Early History of Sexual Art," in *Primitive Erotic Art*, ed. Phillip Rawson (New York: G. P. Putnam, 1973), 8.

3. Sigfried Giedion, *The Eternal Present*. Vol. 1: *The Beginnings of Art* (New York: Pantheon, 1962), 173.

4. Henri Delporte, *L'Image de la femme dans l'art préhistorique* (Paris: Picard, 1979), 47, trans. W. M. L.

5. Giedion, *Eternal Present*, 178.

6. Alexander Marshack, *The Roots of Civilization* (New York: McGraw-Hill, 1972), 279.

7. Marija Gimbutas, *The Language of the Goddess: Unearthing the Hidden Symbols of Western Civilization* (San Francisco: Harper and Row, 1989), 102.

8. Marshack, *Roots*, 293–94.

9. Rawson, "Early History of Sexual Art," 18.

10. Giedion, *Eternal Present*, 173.

11. Marshack, *Roots*, 305.

12. Marshack, *Roots*, 335, n. 17.

13. Marshack, *Roots*, 335.

14. William Irwin Thompson, *The Time Falling Bodies Take to Light: Mythology, Sexuality, and the Origins of Culture* (New York: St. Martin's, 1981), 105.

15. Marija Gimbutas, *Language* (San Francisco: Harper and Row, 1989), 316.

16. Gimbutas, *Language*, 259, caption for fig. 406.

17. Dragoslav Srejović, *Europe's First Monumental Sculpture: New Discoveries at Lepenski Vir*, trans. Lovett F. Edwards (New York: Stein and Day, 1972), 112.

18. Srejoviç, 103.

19. Gimbutas, *Language*, 260.

20. Srejović, *Sculpture*, 113.

21. Srejović, *Sculpture*, 83–84.

22. Srejović, *Sculpture*, 124.

23. Gimbutas, *Language*, 260.

24. Gimbutas, *Language*, 40.

25. Marshack, *Roots*, 313.

CHAPTER 7. SACRED OR PROFANE?

1. Roberto Calasso, *The Marriage of Cadmus and Harmony* (New York: Knopf, 1993), 279.

2. Erich Neumann, *The Great Mother* (New York: Pantheon, 1963), 114–15.

3. Margaret A. Murray, "Female Fertility Figures," *Journal of the Royal Anthropological Institute of Great Britain and Ireland* 64 (1934): 94.

4. Murray, "Female Fertility Figures," 94.

5. Marija Gimbutas, *The Language of the Goddess: Unearthing the Hidden Symbols of Western Civilization.* (San Francisco: Harper and Row, 1989), 253.

6. Marija Gimbutas, *The Goddesses and Gods of Old Europe* (Berkeley: University of California Press, 1982), 176–77.

7. Gimbutas, *Language*, 251.

8. Gimbutas, *Language,*, 256.

9. Peter Lacovara, *Mummies and Magic: The Funerary Arts of Ancient Egypt* (Boston: Museum of Fine Arts, 1988), 127.

10. Maurice Olender, "Aspects de Baubô: Textes et contextes antiques," *Revue de l'histoire des religions* 202 (1985): 46–47, trans. W. M. L.

11. Wendy Doniger, *Other Peoples' Myths: The Cave of Echoes* (New York: Macmillan, 1988), 129.

12. Doniger, *Other Peoples' Myths*, 146.

13. Mircea Eliade, *A History of Religious Ideas.* Vol 1.: *From the Stone Age to the Eleusinian Mysteries*, trans. Willard R. Trask (Chicago: University of Chicago Press, 1978), 27.

CHAPTER 8. METAMORPHOSIS TO MONSTER

1. From Adrienne Rich, "Planetarium," in *Collected Early Poems: 1950–1970* (New York: Norton, 1993), 361 (by permission of the author).

2. R. Gordon Wasson, Albert Hofman, and Carl A. P. Ruck, *The Road to Eleusis: Unveiling the Secret of the Mysteries* (New York: Harcourt Brace Jovanovich, 1978), 111.

3. Wendy Doniger, *Other Peoples' Myths: The Cave of Echoes* (New York: Macmillan, 1988), 71.

4. Doniger, *Other Peoples' Myths*, 71.

5. Eva C. Keuls, *The Reign of the Phallus: Sexual Politics in Ancient Athens* (New York: Harper and Row, 1985), 3.

6. George D. Thomson, *The Prehistoric Aegean* (London: Lawrence and Wishart, 1949), 145.

7. Hesiod, *Theogony*, in *Hesiod, The Homeric Poems, and Homerica*, ed, Hugh G. Evelyn-White (1914; reprint, Cambridge, Mass.: Harvard University Press, 1964), line 279, p. 98.

8. Robert Graves, *The Greek Myths* (New York: Penguin, 1955), 1: 244, n. 6. Some authorities now disagree with Graves and believe that there is no evidence for a matriarchal society at this date.

9. Miriam Robbins Dexter, *Whence the Goddesses: A Source Book* (New York: Pergamon, 1990), 143.

10. Angelo Procopiou, "The True Face of Medusa," trans. Kay Cicellis, *Greek Heritage* 2, no. 6 (1965): 19.

11. Procopiou, "True Face of Medusa," 22.

12. Percy Bysshe Shelley, "On the Medusa of Leonardo da Vinci," in *Complete Poetical Works of Percy Bysshe Shelley*, ed. Thomas Hutchinson (New York: Oxford University Press, 1967), 582–83.

13. Marija Gimbutas, *The Language of the Goddess* (San Francisco: Harper and Row, 1989), 208.

14. Page DuBois, *Sowing the Body: Psychoanalysis and Ancient Representations of Women* (Chicago: University of Chicago Press, 1988), 92.

15. Jean Claire, *Méduse: Contributions à une anthropologie des arts du visuel* (Paris: Éditions Gallimard, 1989), 47, trans. W. M. L.

16. Claire, *Méduse*, 48, trans. W. M. L.

17. Claire, *Méduse*, 49, trans. W. M. L.

CHAPTER 9. THE TRANSFORMER TRANSFORMED

1. Muriel Rukeyser, from "Voices of Waking," in *The Collected Poems of Muriel Rukeyser* (New York: McGraw-Hill, 1978), 419 (by permission of William Rukeyser).

2. *From the Lands of the Scythians, Metropolitan Museum of Art Bulletin*, no. 5 (New York: Metropolitan Museum of Art), plate 65, 108.

3 *Herodotus*, ed. A. D. Godley (Cambridge, Mass.: Harvard University Press, 1920), book 4, sections 17 and 53, 2: 219, 253–55.

4. Excavations of I. E. Zabelin and A. E. Lyutsenko, Hermitage, St. Petersburg, 1864.

5. Paul Perdrizet, *Les Terres cuites Grecques de l'Égypte: De la collection Fouquet* (Paris: Berger-Levrault, 1921), 56.

6. Perdrizet, *Les Terres cuites*, 122, trans. W. M. L.

7. Erich Neumann, *The Great Mother: An Analysis of the Archetype*, trans. Ralph Manheim (New York: Pantheon, 1963), 139.

8. Nor Hall, *The Moon and the Virgin: Reflections on the Archetypal Feminine* (New York: Harper and Row, 1980), 46.

9. Perdrizet, *Les Terres cuites*, 124, trans. W. M. L.

10. Eva C. Keuls, *The Reign of the Phallus: Sexual Politics in Ancient Athens* (New York: Harper and Row, 1985), 353.

11. In addition to *khoiros*=pig, various commonplace names were used by ancient

Greek writers for female genitalia. Jeffrey Henderson, in *The Maculate Muse* (Oxford, 1991), provides other listings: *iskas*=dried fig; *sukon*=fruit of a fig; *kokkos*=pomegranate seed; *rodon*=rose; *keypos*=garden; *hipnos*=oven; *kuklos*=anything circular; *thura*=doorway; *opey*=mousehole; *kogchey*=a cockle sea shell; *kolpos*=a hollow place, fold of garment, or bosom; and *kuown*=dog, commonly used for the sex organs of both women and men. Page DuBois in *Sowing the Body* discusses other metaphors.

12. Marija Gimbutas, *The Language of the Goddess: Unearthing the Hidden Symbols of Western Civilization* (San Francisco: Harper and Row, 1989), 146.

13. Johann Wolfgang von Goethe, *Faust*, Part One, trans. Philip Wayne (New York: Penguin, 1983), 171.

14. "Apis," in *Larousse Encyclopedia of Mythology* (New York: Prometheus, 1959), 44.

15. Perdrizet, *Les Terres cuites*, 55, trans. W. M. L.

16. Ibid.

17. Jean Claire, *Méduse: Contributions à une anthropologie des arts du visuel* (Paris: Éditions Gallimard, 1989), 44–45, trans. W. M. L.

CHAPTER 10. BAUBO MEETS HER DARK SISTERS

1. Margaret R. Miles, *Carnal Knowing: Female Nakedness and Religious Meaning in the Christian West* (Boston: Beacon, 1989), 151.

2. Miles, *Carnal Knowing*, 144.

3. Miles, *Carnal Knowing*, 152.

4. Miles, *Carnal Knowing*, 152.

5. Miles, *Carnal Knowing*, 153.

6. Margaret A. Murray, "Female Fertility Figures," *Journal of the Royal Anthropological Institute of Great Britain and Ireland* 64 (1934): 97.

7. Barbara Walker, *The Woman's Encyclopedia of Myths and Secrets* (New York: Harper and Row, 1983), 931–32.

8. Merlin Stone, *When God Was a Woman* (New York: Harcourt Brace Jovanovich, 1976), 158.

9. Lawrence Durdin-Robertson, *The Goddesses of Chaldea, Syria and Egypt* (Enniscorthy, Eire: Cesara, 1975), 98. Miriam Robbins Dexter, in reviewing the manuscript for this book, recently brought to my attention that *shee*, as in *banshee*, comes from the Old Irish *sid*, a fairy mound, and that *ban* is a combining form from *ben*, meaning *woman*. Thus, a banshee is a female fairy, a woman of the fairy mound.

10. From Thomas Wright *The Worship of the Generative Powers During the Middle Ages in Western Europe* (1866), in Richard Payne Knight and Thomas Wright, *Sexual Symbolism: A History of Phallic Worship* (1866; reprint, New York: Julian Press, 1957), 36.

11. Anne Ross, "Celtic Northern Art," in Philip S. Rawson, ed., *Primitive Erotic Art* (New York: G. P. Putnam, 1973), 104.

12. Ross, "Celtic Northern Art," 105.

13. Murray, "Female Fertility Figures," 99.

14. Murray, "Female Fertility Figures," 99.

15. Anthony Weir and James Jerman, *Images of Lust* (London: Batsford, 1988).

16. Jorgen Andersen, *The Witch on the Wall: Medieval Erotic Sculpture in the British Isles* (London: George Allen, 1977), 48.

17. Andersen, *Witch*, 134.

18. Andersen, *Witch*, 121.

19. Andersen, *Witch*, 133.

20. George Devereux, *Baubo, la vulve mythique* (Paris: Jean-Cyrille Godefroy, 1983), 190–91, trans. W. M. L.

21. Heinrich Kramer and Jakob Sprenger, *Malleus Maleficarum*, ed. and trans. Montague Summers (New York: Dover, 1971), 44–47.

22. Barbara Ehrenreich and Dierdre English, *For Her Own Good: 150 Years of the Experts' Advice to Women* (Garden City, N.Y.: Doubleday, 1979), 35.

23. William Irwin Thompson, *The Time Falling Bodies Take to Light: Mythology, Sexuality, and the Origins of Culture* (New York: St. Martin's, 1981), 165.

CHAPTER II. THE SHE AND THE HE OF IT

1. Peggy Reeves Sanday, *Female Power and Male Dominance: On the Origins of Sexual Inequality* (New York: Cambridge University Press, 1981), 186.

2. Walter Burkert, *Structure and History in Greek Mythology and Ritual* (Berkeley: University of California Press, 1979), 40.

3. Burkert, *Structure and History*, 40.

4. George Thomson, *The Prehistoric Aegean* (London: Lawrence and Wishart, 1978), 173.

5. *Herodotus*, ed. A. D. Godley (Cambridge, Mass.: Harvard University Press, 1920), book 2, sections 50, 51, 1: 338.

6. Norman O. Brown, *Hermes, The Thief: The Evolution of a Myth* (1947; reprint,

Hudson, N. Y.: Lindisfarne Press, 1990), 131. In Brown's opinion, the *Hymn to Hermes* was not written in the seventh century but considerably later, nor was it written for a religious occasion. It was more probably composed for a private festival or banquet given at the court of Hipparchus. Brown therefore sets the date at 520 to 511 BCE.

7. Walter Otto, *The Homeric Gods: The Spiritual Significance of Greek Religion*, trans. Moses Hadas (New York: Pantheon, 1954), 104–5.

8. Hecate was a Titaness, one of the archaic Greek Deities who preceded the Olympians. She was also a chthonian goddess known for her skills in nocturnal sorcery and her powers of regeneration; for she gave life and took it away again. In the Homeric *Hymn to Demeter*, Hecate was the first to hear the shrieks of the abducted girl. When Persephone eventually returned to her mother on earth, Hecate was there to greet her and remained a close and devoted attendant for the young Queen of Hades on her yearly journey. This is the same role accorded Baubo Chthonius by the Orphic poets.

9. Brown, *Hermes*, 14.

10. Brown, *Hermes*, 43.

11. Brown, *Hermes*, 38.

12. From Thomas Wright, *The Worship of the Generative Powers During the Middle Ages in Western Europe* (1866), in Richard Payne Knight and Thomas Wright, *Sexual Symbolism: A History of Phallic Worship* (1866; reprint, New York: Julian Press, 1957), plate III, p. 37.

13. Margaret A. Murray, "Female Fertility Figures," *Journal of the Royal Anthropological Institute of Great Britain and Ireland* 64 (1934): 98.

14. Mircea Eliade, *Myths, Dreams, and Mysteries: The Encounter between Contemporary Faiths and Archaic Realities*, trans. Philip Mairet (New York: Harper, 1960), 145.

15. Virginia Woolf, *A Room of One's Own* (New York: Penguin, 1963), 102.

16. Ajit Mookerjee, *Kali, The Feminine Force* (London: Thames and Hudson, 1988), 27.

APPENDIX I. HOMERIC *HYMN TO DEMETER*

1. Fragment of a Mycenean vase, circa 1300–1270 BCE, based on William, Lord Taylour, *The Mycenaeans* (London: Thames and Hudson, 1964), p. 136, fig. 123.

2. All quotations have been translated by W. M. L. and are based on the Greek text from the *Hymn to Demeter*, in *Hesiod, The Homeric Poems, and Homerica*, ed. Hugh G. Evelyn-White (1914; reprint, Cambridge, Mass.: Harvard University Press, 1964), 288–324.

APPENDIX 2. A SELECTION OF MYTHS REFLECTING THE SPIRIT OF BAUBO

1. Original woodcut design by W. M. L.

2. William Irwin Thompson, *The Time Falling Bodies Take to Light: Mythology, Sexuality, and the Origins of Culture* (New York: St. Martin's, 1981), 213.

3. Thompson, *Falling Bodies*, 237.

4. James G. MacQueen, *The Hittites and Their Contemporaries in Asia Minor* (London: Thames and Hudson, 1986), 110.

5. Hans G. Güterbock, "Hittite Mythology," in Samuel N. Kramer, ed., *Mythologies of the Ancient World* (Garden City, N. Y.: Doubleday, 1961). All quotations in this synopsis are from Güterbock's translation of the ancient clay tablets.

6. Lawrence Durdin-Robertson, *The Goddesses of Chaldea, Syria and Egypt* (Enniscorthy, Eire: Cesara, 1975), 114.

7. Miriam Robbins Dexter, *Whence the Goddesses: A Source Book* (New York: Pergamon, 1990), 19.

8. Dexter, *Whence the Goddesses*, 21.

9. Diane Wolkstein and Samuel N. Kramer, *Inanna, Queen of Heaven and Earth: Her Stories and Hymns from Sumer* (New York: Harper and Row, 1983), 69.

10. Robert Thomas Rundle Clarke, *Myth and Symbol in Ancient Egypt* (London: Thames and Hudson, 1959), 263.

11. Clarke, *Myths and Symbols*, 80.

12. Merlin Stone, *Ancient Mirrors of Womanhood: A Treasury of Goddess and Heroine Lore from Around the World* (Boston: Beacon, 1979), 272.

13. Clarke, *Myth and Symbol*, 181.

14. Alan H. Gardiner, *The Library of A. Chester Beatty: Description of a Hieratic Papyrus* (New York: Oxford University Press, 1931), 16. All quotations are from Gardiner's rendering of the Beatty Papyrus in this source.

15. Gardiner, 16n.

16. Clarke, *Myth and Symbol*, 199.

17. Clarke, *Myth and Symbol*, 231.

18. A number of discussions of and sources for the myth of Amaterasu are available to the English-speaking reader, among them: Mircea Eliade, *From Primitives to Zen: A Thematic Sourcebook of the History of Religions* (London: Collins, 1967); Dale Saunders, "Japanese Mythology," in *Mythologies of the Ancient World*, ed. Samuel N. Kramer (Garden City, N.Y.: Doubleday, 1961); "The Significance of Amaterasu in Japanese Religion; Religious History for Nakamura, Motomiechi, Kyoko," in Carl

Olson, ed., *The Book of the Goddess, Past and Present: An Introdution to Her Religion*, (New York: Crossroad, 1983); Juliet Piggot, *Japanese Mythology* (Feltham, N.Y.: P. Hamlyn, 1969); and Merlin Stone, *Ancient Mirrors of Womanhood* (Boston: Beacon, 1979).

19. Mariflor Parpan, videotaped interview at the Non-Governmental Forum, Nairobi, Kenya, 1985 (Cambridge, Mass.: Women's Video Collective, 1986). All quotations have been transcribed from this source by W. M. L. This conference was a women's alternative to the contemporaneous U.N. conference in Nairobi, which forum organizers asserted was male dominated and out of touch with women's issues.

20. "The Bravery of Women," in *Plutarch's Moralia*, trans. Frank Babbitt Cole et al., vol. 3 (Cambridge, Mass.: Harvard University Press, 1931), 5.246a.

21. Ibid. 4.248.

22. This is from a version of the ancient tale by Táin Bo Cuailnge, written circa 1186–1192 and recorded in Dexter, *Whence the Goddesses*, 160. My thanks to Miriam Robbins Dexter for drawing my attention to the Bellerophon and the Cú Chulainn myths.

BIBLIOGRAPHY

Andersen, Jorgen. *The Witch on the Wall: Medieval Erotic Sculpture in the British Isles.* London: George Allen, 1977.

Aristophanes. *The Frogs.* Trans. David Barrett. New York: Penguin, 1964.

Atwood, Margaret. *Two-Headed Poems.* New York: Oxford University Press, 1978.

Beati, Sancti a Liebana. *In Apocalypsin, Codex Gerundensis.* 2 vols. Laussane: Urs Graf-Verlag, 1962.

Boardman, John. *Athenian Red Figure Vases: The Archaic Period.* London: Thames and Hudson, 1985.

Bossert, Helmut Theodor. *The Art of Ancient Crete from the Earliest Times to the Iron Age.* London: Zwemmer, 1937.

Bowra, Cecil M., ed. *Oxford Book of Greek Verse.* Oxford: Clarendon Press, 1938.

Brody, J. J. *Mimbres Painted Pottery.* Sante Fe, N. Mex.: School of American Research, 1977.

Brown, Norman O. *Hermes, The Thief: The Evolution of a Myth.* 1947. Reprint. Hudson, N.Y.: Lindisfarne Press, 1990.

Brumfield, Allaire Chandler. *The Attic Festivals of Demeter and Their Relation to the Agricultural Year.* Salem, N.H.: Ayer, 1981.

Budge, Ernest Alfred. *The Gods of the Egyptians: Studies in Egyptian Mythology.* 2 vols. 1904. Reprint. New York: Dover, 1969.

Burkert, Walter. *Greek Religion.* Trans. John Raffar. Cambridge, Mass.: Harvard University Press, 1985.

——. *Structure and History in Greek Mythology and Ritual.* Berkeley: University of California Press, 1979.

Burland, Cottie A., ed. *Magic Books from Mexico.* Harmondsworth, England: Penguin, 1953.

Callimachus. "To Demeter." In *Callimachus, Lycophron, Aratus.* Ed. and trans. A. W. Mair and G. R. Mair. 1921. Reprint. Cambridge, Mass.: Harvard University Press, 1977.

Calasso, Roberto. *The Marriage of Cadmus and Harmony.* New York: Knopf, 1993.

Chamoux, François. *The Civilization of Greece.* Trans. W. S. Maguinness. New York: Simon and Schuster, 1965.

Claire, Jean. *Méduse: Contributions à une anthropologie des arts du visuel.* Paris: Éditions Gallimard, 1989.

Clarke, Robert Thomas Rundle. *Myth and Symbol in Ancient Egypt.* London: Thames and Hudson, 1959.

Clement of Alexandria. *Protrepticos (Exhortation to the Greeks),* in *Clement of Alexandria.* Ed. G. W. Butterworth. New York: G. P. Putnam, 1919.

Debrida, Bella. "Drawing from Mythology on Women's Quest for Selfhood." In *The Politics of Women's Spirituality.* Ed. Charlene Spretnak. New York: Doubleday, 1982.

Delporte, Henri. *L'Image de la femme dans l'art préhistorique.* Paris: Picard, 1979.

Devambez, Pierre. *Greek Painting.* Trans. Jean Stewart. New York: Viking, 1962.

Devereux, George. *Baubo, la vulve mythique.* Paris: Jean-Cyrille Godefroy, 1983.

Dexter, Miriam Robbins. *Whence the Goddesses: A Source Book.* New York: Pergamon, 1990.

Diodorus Siculus. *Didorus of Sicily.* Vol. 1. Trans. C. H. Oldfather. New York: G. P. Putnam, 1933.

Dodds, Eric Robertson. *The Greeks and the Irrational.* Berkeley: University of California Press, 1951.

Doniger, Wendy. *Other Peoples' Myths: The Cave of Echoes.* New York: Macmillan, 1988.

DuBois, Page. *Sowing the Body: Psychoanalysis and Ancient Representations of Women.* Chicago: University of Chicago Press, 1988.

Duby, George. *The Age of the Cathedrals: Art and Society, 980–1420.* Trans. Eleanor Devieux and Barbara Thompson. Chicago: University of Chicago Press, 1981.

Duerr, Hans Peter. *Dreamtime: Concerning the Boundary between Wilderness and Civilization.* Trans. Felicitas Goodman. New York: Basil Blackwell, 1985.

Durdin-Robertson, Lawrence. *The Goddesses of Chaldea, Syria and Egypt.* Enniscorthy, Eire: Cesara, 1975.

Ehrenreich, Barbara, and Dierdre English. *For Her Own Good: 150 Years of the Experts' Advice to Women.* Garden City, N.Y.: Doubleday, 1979.

Eisler, Riane. *The Chalice and the Blade.* New York: Harper and Row, 1987.

Eliade, Mircea. *A History of Religious Ideas.* Vol. 1: *From the Stone Age to the Eleusinian Mysteries.* Trans. Willard R. Trask. Chicago: University of Chicago Press, 1978.

——. *Myths, Dreams and Mysteries: The Encounter between Contemporary Faiths and Archaic Realities.* Trans. Philip Mairet. New York: Harper, 1960.

——. *Patterns in Comparative Religion.* New York: Sheed and Ward, 1958.

Encyclopédie photographique de l'art. Paris: Éditions "Tel," 1936–49.

Estés, Clarissa Pinkola. *Women Who Run with the Wolves: Myths and Stories of the Wild Woman Archetype.* New York: Ballantine, 1992.

Feldman, Thalia. *Gorgo and the Origins of Fear.* San Francisco: Arion, 1965.

Fitzhugh, William W., and Aron Crowell, eds. *Crossroads of Continents: Cultures of Siberia and Alaska.* Washington, D.C.: Smithsonian Institution, 1988.

Friedrich, Paul. *The Meaning of Aphrodite.* Chicago: University of Chicago Press, 1978.

From the Land of the Scythians. Metropolitan Museum of Art Bulletin, no. 5, 1973–74. Catalogue of exhibit, The Metropolitan Museum of Art, New York, and the Los Angeles County Museum of Art.

Gardiner, Alan H. *The Library of A. Chester Beatty: Description of a Hieratic Papyrus.* Oxford: Oxford University Press, 1931.

Giedion, Sigfried. *The Eternal Present.* Vol. 1: *The Beginnings of Art.* New York: Pantheon, 1962.

——. *Sign, Image and Symbol.* Ed. Georgy Kepes. New York: George Braziller, 1966.

Gimbutas, Marija. *The Goddesses and Gods of Old Europe.* Berkeley: University of California Press, 1982.

——. *The Language of the Goddess: Unearthing the Hidden Symbols of Western Civilization.* San Francisco: Harper and Row, 1989.

Goethe, Johann Wolfgang von. *Faust,* Part One. Trans. Philip Wayne. New York: Penguin, 1983.

——. "On Morphology." In *Goethe's Botanical Writings.* Trans. Bertha Mueller. Honolulu: University of Hawaii Press, 1952.

Graves, Robert. *The Greek Myths.* 2 vols. New York: Penguin, 1955.

Guthrie, William K. C. *Orpheus and Greek Religion: A Study of the Orphic Movement.* 1952. Reprint. New York: Norton, 1966.

Hall, Nor. *The Moon and the Virgin: Reflections on the Archetypal Feminine.* New York: Harper and Row, 1980.

Halperin, David M., John J. Winkler, and Froma I. Zeitlin, eds. *Before Sexuality: The Construction of Erotic Experience in the Ancient Greek World.* Princeton, N.J.: Princeton University Press, 1990.

Harding, Esther M. *Women's Mysteries.* New York: Pantheon, 1955.

Harrison, Jane Ellen. *Prolegomena to the Study of Greek Religion.* 1903. Reprint. London: Merlin Press, 1980.

——. *Themis: A Study of the Social Origins of Greek Religion.* In *Epilegomena . . . and Themis. . . .* New Hyde Park, N.Y.: University Books, 1962.

Hawkes, Jacquetta. *The Dawn of the Gods.* New York: Random House, 1968.

Hawkes, Jacquetta, and Leonard Wooley. *Prehistory and the Beginnings of Civilization.* New York: Harper, 1963.

Herodotus. *Herodotus.* Ed. and trans. A. D. Godley. Cambridge, Mass.: Harvard University Press, 1920.

Hesiod. *Theogony.* In *Hesiod, The Homeric Hymns, and Homerica.* Trans. Hugh G. Evelyn-White. 1914. Reprint. Cambridge, Mass.: Harvard University Press, 1964.

The Human Figure in Early Greek Art. Catalogue of exhibit, National Gallery of Art, Washington, D.C., 1988.

Hymn to Demeter. In *Hesiod, The Homeric Hymns, and Homerica.* Trans. Hugh G. Evelyn-White. Cambridge, Mass.: Harvard University Press, 1977.

Ions, Veronica. *Egyptian Mythology.* London: Hamlyn, 1975.

Jung, Carl G., and Karl Kerenyi. *Essays on a Science of Mythology: The Myth of the Divine Child and the Mysteries of Eleusis.* Princeton, N.J.: Princeton University Press, 1949.

Keller, Mara Lynn. "The Elusinian Mysteries of Demeter and Persephone: Fertility, Sexuality and Rebirth." *Journal of Feminist Studies in Religion* 4 (Spring 1988): 27–54.

Kerenyi, Karl. *Eleusis: Archetypal Image of Mother and Daughter.* Trans. Ralph Manheim. Princeton, N.J.: Princeton University Press, 1967.

——. *The Gods of the Greeks.* London: Thames and Hudson, 1951.

——. *Zeus and Hera: Archetypal Image of Father, Husband and Wife.* Trans. Christopher Holme. Princeton, N.J.: Princeton University Press, 1975.

Keuls, Eva C. *The Reign of the Phallus: Sexual Politics in Ancient Athens.* New York: Harper and Row, 1985.

Kirk, Geoffrey Stephen. *Myth: Its Meaning and Functions in Ancient and Other Cultures.* Cambridge, England: Cambridge University Press; Berkeley: University of California Press, 1970.

——. *The Nature of Greek Myths.* New York: Penguin, 1974.

Kramer, Heinrich, and Jakob Sprenger. *Malleus Maleficarum.* Trans. Montague Summers. New York: Dover, 1971.

Kramer, Samuel N., ed. *Mythologies of the Ancient World.* Garden City, N.Y.: Doubleday, 1961.

Lacovara, Peter. *Mummies and Magic: The Funerary Arts of Ancient Egypt.* Boston: Museum of Fine Arts, 1988.

Larousse Encyclopedia of Mythology. New York: Prometheus, 1959.

Lefkowitz, Mary R., and Maureen B. Fant, eds. *Women's Life in Greece and Rome.* Baltimore: The Johns Hopkins University Press, 1982.

Lerner, Gerda. *The Creation of Patriarchy.* New York: Oxford University Press, 1986.

Lévêque, Pierre. *The Greek Adventure.* Cleveland: World, 1968.

Levertov, Denise. *The Jacob's Ladder.* New York: New Directions, 1961.

Lincoln, Bruce. *Emerging from the Chrysalis: Studies in Rituals of Women's Initiation.* Cambridge, Mass.: Harvard University Press, 1981.

Lurker, Manfred. *Dictionary of Gods and Goddesses, Devils and Demons.* Trans. G. L. Campbell. London: Routledge and Kegan Paul, 1987.

Macqueen, James G. *The Hittites and Their Contemporaries in Asia Minor.* London: Thames and Hudson, 1986.

Marshack, Alexander. *The Roots of Civilization.* New York: McGraw-Hill, 1972.

Mayer, J., and T. N. Prideaux. *Never to Die: The Egyptians in Their Own Words.* New York: Viking, 1938.

Meador, Betty de Shong. "The Thesmophoria: A Women's Ritual." *Psychological Perspectives* 17 (1986): 35–45.

Mellaart, James S. *Çatal Hüyük: A Neolithic Town in Anatolia.* New York: McGraw-Hill, 1967.

Mercier, Jacques. *Ethiopian Magic Scrolls.* New York: George Braziller, 1979.

Miles, Margaret R. *Carnal Knowing: Female Nakedness and Religious Meaning in the Christian West.* Boston: Beacon, 1989.

Milton, John. *Paradise Lost.* New York: Odyssey, 1962.

Mookerjee, Ajit. *Kali, The Feminine Force.* London: Thames and Hudson, 1988.

Morgan, Robin. *Upstairs in the Garden.* New York: Norton, 1990.

Murray, Henry A., ed. *Myth and Mythmaking.* New York: George Braziller, 1960.

Murray, Margaret A. "Female Fertility Figures." *Journal of the Royal Anthropological Institute of Great Britain and Ireland* 64 (1934): 93–100.

Mylonas, George, *Eleusis and the Eleusinian Mysteries.* Princeton, N.J.: Princeton University Press, 1972.

Neumann, Erich. *The Great Mother: An Analysis of the Archetype.* Trans. Ralph Manheim. New York: Pantheon, 1963.

Nietzsche, Friedrich. *Nietzsche Contra Wagner.* In *The Portable Nietzsche.* Ed. and trans. Walter Kaufmann. New York: Viking, 1954.

Olender, Maurice. "Aspects de Baubô: Textes et contextes antiques." *Revue de l'histoire des religions* 202 (1985): 3–55.

——. "Baubo," s.v. *Encyclopedia of Religion.* 16 vols. Ed. Mircea Eliade et al. New York: Macmillan, 1987.

Olson, Carl, ed. *The Book of the Goddess, Past and Present: An Introduction to her Religion.* New York: Crossroad, 1987.

Otto, Walter. *The Homeric Gods: The Spiritual Significance of Greek Religion.* Trans. Moses Hadas. New York: Pantheon, 1954.

Padel, Ruth. "Model for Possession by Greek Daemons." In *Images of Women in Antiquity,* ed. Averil Cameron and Amelie Kuhrt. Detroit: Wayne State University Press, 1983.

Paris, Ginette. *Pagan Meditations: The Worlds of Aphrodite, Artemis and Hestia.* Trans. Gwendolyn Moore. East Lansing, Mich.: Spring, 1986.

Parpan, Mariflor. Videotape interview at Women's Non-Governmental Organization Forum, Nairobi, Kenya. Cambridge, Mass.: Women's Video Collective, 1986.

Parrot, Andre. *Sumer, The Dawn of Art.* Trans. Stuart Gilbert and James Emmons. New York: Golden Press, 1961.

Perdrizet, Paul. *Bronzes Grecs de l'Égypte de la collection Fouquet.* Paris: Berger-Levrault, 1911.

——. *Les Terres cuites Grecques de l'Égypte de la collection Fouquet.* Paris: Berger-Levrault, 1921.

Picard, Charles. "L'Épisode de Baubô dans les Mystères d'Eleusis." *Revue de l'histoire des religions* 95 (1927): 220–55.

Piggott, Juliet. *Japanese Mythology.* Feltham, N.Y.: P. Hamlyn, 1969.

Plutarch, "The Bravery of Women." In *Plutarch's Moralia: In Seventeen Volumes.* Trans. Frank Babbitt Cole et al. Vol. 3. Cambridge, Mass.: Harvard University Press, 1931.

Pomeroy, Sarah B. *Goddesses, Whores, Wives and Slaves: Women in Classical Antiquity.* New York: Schocken, 1975.

Procopiou, Angelo. "The True Face of Medusa." Trans. Kay Cicellis. *Greek Heritage* 2, no. 6 (1965): 16–24.

Rawson, Phillip. "Early History of Sexual Art." In *Primitive Erotic Art,* ed. Phillip Rawson. New York: G. P. Putnam, 1973.

Rich, Adrienne. *On Lies, Secrets and Silence: Selected Prose, 1966–1978.* New York: Norton, 1979.

——. *Collected Early Poems, 1950–1970.* New York: Norton, 1993.

Richardson, Nicholas, ed. *The Homeric Hymn to Demeter.* New York: Oxford University Press, 1974.

Ross, Anne. "Celtic Northern Art." In *Primitive Erotic Art,* ed. Phillip Rawson. New York: G. P. Putnam, 1973.

Rudner, Jalmar, and Ione Rudner. *The Hunter and His Art: A Survey of Rock Art in Southern Africa.* Cape Town: C. Struik, 1970.

Rukeyser, Muriel. *The Collected Poems of Muriel Rukeyser.* New York: McGraw-Hill, 1978.

Salvini, Roberto. *Wiligelmo e le Origini della Scultura Romanica.* Milano: Aldo Martello Editore, 1956.

Sanday, Peggy Reeves. *Female Power and Male Dominance: On the Origins of Sexual Inequality.* New York: Cambridge University Press, 1981.

Shelley, Percy Bysshe. "On the Medusa of Leonardo da Vinci." In *Complete Poetical Works of Percy Bysshe Shelley*, ed. Thomas Hutchinson. New York: Oxford University Press, 1967.

Shuttle, Penelope, and Peter Redgrave. *The Wise Wound: Myths, Realities and Meanings of Menstruation.* New York: Grove Weidenfeld, 1988.

Simpson, Jacqueline, ed. *European Mythology: Library of the World's Myths and Legends.* New York: Peter Bedric, 1987.

Slater, Philip E. *The Glory of Hera: Greek Mythology and the Greek Family.* Boston: Beacon, 1971.

Srejović, Dragoslav. *Europe's First Monumental Sculpture: New Discoveries at Lepenski Vir.* Trans. Lovett F. Edwards. New York: Stein and Day, 1972.

Stone, Merlin. *Ancient Mirrors of Womanhood: A Treasury of Goddess and Heroine Lore From Around the World.* Boston: Beacon, 1979.

——. *When God Was a Woman.* New York: Harcourt Brace Jovanovich, 1976.

Stroud, Ronald, and Nancy Bookidis. *Demeter and Persephone in Ancient Corinth.* Princeton, N. J.: American School of Classical Studies at Athens, Corinth Notes, no. 2, 1987.

Taylour, William, Lord . *The Mycenaeans.* London: Thames and Hudson, 1964.

Thompson, William Irwin. *Darkness and Scattered Light.* Garden City, N.Y.: Doubleday, 1978.

——. *Evil and World Order.* New York: Harper and Row, 1976.

——. *The Time Falling Bodies Take to Light: Mythology, Sexuality, and the Origins of Culture.* New York: St. Martin's, 1981.

Thomson, George D. *The Prehistoric Aegean.* London: Lawrence and Wishart, 1949.

Vezin, Gilberte. *L'Apocalypse et la fin des temps.* Paris: Éditions de la revue moderne, 1973.

Vaufrey, R. "L'Age de l'art rupestre nord-Africaine." *Cahiers d'art* (1937): 63–77.

Waetzoldt, Wilhelm. *Durer and his Times.* Trans. R. H. Boothroyd. London: Phaidon, 1950.

Walker, Barbara. *The Woman's Encyclopedia of Myths and Secrets.* New York: Harper and Row, 1983.

Wasson, R. Gordon, Albert Hofman, and Carl A. P. Ruck. *The Road to Eleusis: Unveiling the Secret of the Mysteries.* New York: Harcourt Brace Jovanovich, 1978.

Weir, Anthony, and James Jerman. *Images of Lust.* London: Batsford, 1988.

White, Randall. *Dark Caves, Bright Visions: Life in Ice Age Europe.* New York: Norton, 1986.

Whitmont, Edward C. *Return of The Goddess.* New York: Crossroad, 1982.

Woldering, Irmgard. *The Art of Egypt.* New York: Crown, 1963.

Wolkstein, Diane, and Samuel N. Kramer. *Inanna, Queen of Heaven and Earth: Her Stories and Hymns from Sumer.* New York: Harper and Row, 1983.

Wooley, Leonard C. *The Sumerians.* New York: Norton, 1965.

Woolf, Virginia. *A Room of One's Own.* New York: Penguin, 1963.

Wright, Thomas. *The Worship of the Generative Powers During the Middle Ages in Western Europe.* In Richard Payne Knight and Thomas Wright, *Sexual Symbolism: A History of Phallic Worship.* 1866. Reprint. New York: Julian Press, 1957.

INDEX

Page references in italics signify illustrations.

Abba Samuel, 136–37, *138*

Abri Cellier, *58*, 59

Achilles, 104

Acrocorinth, 11

Adam, 129, 131

Aegean artifacts, 21–22, 77

Aegean myths, 168

Aegis of Athena, 108–*9*

African rituals, *10*, 65

Agnuscastus bush, 38

Agrarian rites, 5, *6*, 27, 49

Aideomai, 105, 111

Aischrologia, 36–37, 40, 45, 51

Alaska, 125

Alexander the Great, 115

Alexandrian statuary, *9*, 117, *118*, *119*, 120

Altamira cave, 57

Ama-no-Uzume, 168, 180

Amaterasu, 168, 179–81

Amaunet. See Hathor

Amphora, *149*

Amulets, 77, 79, 95–96, 157, *158*

Ana-suromai, 4, 17, 30, *35*, 84, 152, 177;
defined, 1; Devereux on, 53–54;
Egyptian versions of, 26–27, 117, 123,
168; Japanese version of, 180; modern
survivals of, 20; Olender on, 8;
Philippine version of, 182–84;
Plutarch on, 184

Anasazi frog ornament, 91, *93*

Anat, 24

Anatolia, 91, *94*, 168

Andersen, Jorgen, 143–44

Androcentric cultures. *See* Male
dominance

Androgyny, *64*–65, 135, 157, *158*, 178

L'Angle-sur-L'Anglin, 61, *62*

Animal bones, 76

Animal imagery, 59, *86*–87, 96, 122–23

Ankh symbol, 96

Antler bone carvings, 63, *64*, 65

Aphrodite, xvii, 45, 47, 117

Aphrodite of Cnidus (Praxiteles), 105

Apis, 27, 123, *124*

Apocalypse (New Testament book), 130,
131, 135–37

Apollo, 150

Apollodorus, 107–8

Arcadia, 150

Ardhanarîsvara, 157, *158*

Ares, 104

Argive myths, 107, 108

Aristophanes, 33, 39

Arm position, 84–86, 178

Art materials, 103–4

Artistic conventions, 104–5

Ashmunikal, 169

"Aspects de Baubô" (Olender), 48–49

Athena, xvii, 107, 108–9

Athens: families of, 17; religion of, 42,
107, 108; statuary of, 147–48, 151;
theater of, 39; vase painting of, 98, *99*,
101, 104–5; women of, 41

Attic Greece: art of, 117, 125, 147–48; festivals of, xv, 8, 28, 29–43, 45, 50, 51; poetry of, 15; sexual polarization of, 42, 105; theater of, 12

Attis, 50

Atum, 174, 175, 176, 177, 178

Atwood, Margaret, 21

Azov, Sea of, 114–15

Ba'al, 24

Baalat, 24

Baba, 177

Babylonian deities, *xvi*, 22–24, 87–*88*, 111

Bachofen, Johann Jacob, 46

Baev, 24

Baikal, Lake, 80

Balkan nomads, 30

Banshees, 196 n.9

Baskanos, 125

Bast, 26, 96, 175, 176

Bau, 3, 22–24, 55

Baubo, la vulve mythique (Devereux), 53–54

Baubon, 48, 49

Baubons (artifacts), 189 n.6

"Beatty Papyrus," 176, 177

Beatus (Spanish monk), 135

Bebt, 24

Beersheba bone figurine, *76*

Bellerophon, 184

Bird Goddess, *86*–87

Bird sculpture, 153–*54*

Birthing posture, 88, *89*, 91, *94*, 122

Bisexual imagery. *See* Androgyny

Black Sea, 114–15

Blood imagery (*see also* "Moon blood"; "Wise blood"), 38

Body postures (*see also* Epiphanic gesture; Squatting posture; Upraised arms), 84–97

Boghazkoy (Turkey), 168

Bolivian vulva images, 59, *60*

Bona Dea, 5, 47

Bone carvings, *76*, 77, 83, *90*–*91*; mammoth, 65–*66*, 67, 69, 80; reindeer, 63, *64*, 65

Bravery of Women, 184

Breuil, Henri Édouard Prosper, 57

Brides (*see also* Virgins), 143

British ecclesiastical iconography, 139–44, 154–*55*

Bronze amulets, 157, *158*

Brothels, 41

Bubastis, 26–27, 49, 175

Buddhism, 155

Bull gods, 27, 122–23, 157

Burial sites, 76, 115, 173

Burkert, Walter, 36–37, 51, 150

Butterfly imagery, *126*

Caduceus, 152, 153

Caillech, 141

Calasso, Roberto, 84

Callimachus, 29–30, 33

Callippidae, 115

Cambridgeshire, 154–*55*

Canadian Eskimo carvings, *90*–*91*

Cape Hippolaus, 115

El Castillo, *58*

Castration, 113, 176

Cat goddess, 96, 175, 176

Cathedral iconography, *132*–35

Catholic iconography, 38, 130–46

Cavan County, 141, *142*

Celtic goddesses, 141, 143

"Chaste tree," 38

Chastity (*see also* Virgins), 50

Childbirth posture, 88, *89*, 91, *94*, 122

Chimane Indians, 59, *60*

Christian church, 34–36, 38, 50, 129, 130–31, 130–46, 155

"Chronicles of Japan," 179

Chthonic deities, 30

Chthonius (the word), 152

Church Fathers, 47, 48

Claire, Jean, 111–13, 129

Clay artifacts. *See* Pottery painting; Terra-cotta sculpture; Vase painting

Clay tablets, *32*, 168

Clement of Alexandria, 34, 48, 49, 50, 51, 153

Cleopatra VII, 115

Coffin Texts, 174

Communal menstruation, 38–39

Consolation, 16, 18, 46

Corinth, 11, 12, 41

Cretan frog imagery, 91, *92*

Crimean archeological finds, 114, 115, *116*

Cú Chulainn, 184–85

Cuneiform script, 168

Cybele, 47, 50

Cycladic sculpture, 77, *80*

Cylinder seals, xvi, 87–*88*

Danaus, 36

Danu, 133

Debrida, Bella, 16–17

Delos, 77, *81*, 150, 153

Delporte, Henri, xvi, 61

Demeter (*see also* Demeter-Persephone myth), 3, *19, 32, 35*, 97, *99*; in Aegean inscriptions, 22, 151; arousal of, 53, 54; Callimachus on, 29–30; cult of, 31, 36, 37, 51, 103, 115, 122; in Orphic literature, 18

Demeter and Persephone in Ancient Corinth (Stroud and Bookidis), 11–12

Demeter-Persephone myth, 1, 3–4, 20, 52, 53; Amaterasu myth and, 179, 180; in Athenian vase painting, 98, *99*, 101, 105; in Corinth, 11; Egyptian worship and, 27; in Eleusis, 31–36; *Great Contending* and, 177–78; Hermes Chthonius in, 152; in *Hymn to Demeter*, xv, 13–17, 39–40, 151, 161–65; *Inara and Telipinu* and, 169, 171–72

Demons, 3–4, 35–36, 96, 131, 135, 144, 172–73

Demophoön, 153, 163, 164

Descent of Inanna, 172–73

Devereux, George, 46, 53–54, 101, 120

Devi, 79, 157, *158*

Dexter, Miriam Robbins, 196 n.9

Diels, Hermann, 101

Dildos, 189 n.6

Diodorus Siculus, 26–27, 123

Dionysian worship, 17

Dionysus (*see also* Iacchus), 4

Doniger, Wendy, 97, 103–4

Dordogne, 59, 66

"Dormitory phenomenon," 39

DuBois, Page, 111

Durga, 157

Dysaules, 17, 52

Earth Mother (*see also* Mother Goddess), 52, 108

Ecclesiasticus, 131

Echo, 18

Ecstasy, 42–43

Egypt, 115, 116, 120

Egyptian religion, 24, 26–28, 47, 49, 50, 158, 173–78; animals in, 122–23; frogs in, 91, 94–96; in Hellenistic era, 117–20; Hittite myths and, 169; Perseus myth and, 108; Thesmophoria festival and, 36

Egyptian statuary, *9*, 117, *118*, *119*, 120

Eileithyia, 30

Eleusinian Mysteries, xv, 31–36, 165; Burkert on, 51; Egyptian worship and, 27; Friedrich on, 15–16; Harrison on, 47; *kykeon* in, 164; Mylonas on, 49–50, 103; Olender on, 48–49; Philochorus on, 18; Picard on, 45, 47–48; Psellus on, 3–4; Scythian tomb paintings and, 115

Eleusinian vase painting, *106*

Eleusis, 14, 16, 17, 18, 31, 162

Eliade, Mircea, 97, 155

Empedocles, 4

English ecclesiastical iconography, 139, 143, 144, 154–*55*

Epiphanic gesture, 85, 87, 88

Erech, 139

Eskimo carvings, *90*, 91, 125

Eskimo rituals, 83

Estés, Clarissa Pinkola, 12, 46

Ethiopian scroll, 136–37, *138*

Eubuleus, 17

Euripides, v, 109

Europe: medieval iconography in, 130–46; "Old," 10, 188 n.11; Paleolithic iconography in, 65, 83; toad imagery in, 91, 96; women of, 79

Euryale, 106

Eusebius of Caesarea, 34

Eve, 129, 131

Evil Eye, 49, 125–29, 137

Ex-votos, 120, 124

Exhibitionism. *See* Ana-suromai

Eye of Rê, 174, 175, 176, 177, 178

Far Eastern culture, 155–58

Fasting, 37

Fertile Mother. *See* Mother Goddess

Fertility symbolism, 5, 16, 20; in Egypt, 120; in herms, 150; in Neolithic images, 70; in Paleolithic images, 59, 60; in Sheilahs, 144; in sows, 122; in Thesmophoria festivals, 37

Fish Goddess, 73, *74*, *75*, 76–77

Fouquet, Daniel Marc, 117, 124, 125

French archeological sites, 7, 73; Abri Cellier, *58*, 59; L'Angle-sur-L'Anglin, 61, *62*; La Ferrassie, *58*, 59; Le Gabillou, 61, *63*; Lascaux, 57; Laugerie Basse, 57, 65–*66*; Lespugue, 70–*72*; Le Placard, 63, *64*, 65, 83

French ecclesiastical iconography, 143, 144

Freud, Sigmund, 113

Friedrich, Paul, 15–16

Frog symbolism, 18, 88–*95*, 96–97

The Frogs (Aristophanes), 33

Le Gabillou, 61 *63*

Gaelic legends, 184

Galgenberg Venus figure, *56*, 57, 59

Galla, 172–73

Gardiner, Alan H., 177, 178

Gem seals, *xvi*, 87–*88*

Gender relations, xviii, 42, 79, 104, 105

Genitalia (*see also* Male genitalia; Vagina Dentata; Vulva), 48, 49–50, 51, 65, 104–5, 156–57

Gephyristai, 33

Giedion, Sigried, 59, 61, 66, 101

Gig (the word), 139

Gimbutas, Marija: on the Evil Eye, 125; on Gorgons, 110; on Haçilar artifact, 91; on Lepenski Vir Fish Goddess, 73, 76–77; on Neolithic figures, 70, 73; on "Old Europe," 10, 188 n.11; on Le Placard carving, 65; on sows, 122; on squatting posture, 88, 91; on toads, xiii

"Goddess of Fertility and Fecundity" (Mesopotamian drawing), 86–87

Goethe, Johann Wolfgang von, 46, 122

Gold artifacts, 77, *79, 116*

Golden One (Egyptian deity). *See* Hathor

Gorgo (vulva symbol), 112–13, 129

Gorgons: in art, 110, *111, 166*; in Attic architecture, 148, 150; Evil Eye and, 125; Hesiod on, 106–7; Psellus and, 35

Goths, 35

Grain Goddess. *See* Demeter

Graves, Robert, 46, 108

Great Contending, 176–77

Great Mother Goddess. *See* Mother Goddess

Greece: art of, 98, 101, 117, 125, 147–48; festivals of, xv, 8, 28, 29–43, 45, 50, 51; Hellenistic, 115–17; painting of, *107, 109,* 125, *126, 149*; philosophy of, 174; poetry of, 15, religion of (*see also* Olympian pantheon), 30–31, 41–43, 84; Scythians and, 114–15; women of, 41, 104, 111, 116–17

Grien, Hans Baldung, 145

Gynaeceum, 41

Gynocentric cultures, 11, 28, 30

Gynocide, 145

Haçilar, 91, *94*

Hades (Greek deity), 11, 14, 107, 161, 162, 164–65, 180

Hades (underworld), 17, 152

Hagos (the word), 54

Hall, Nor, 45, 122

Hannahanna, 169, 170, 171, 178

Harding, Esther M., 187 n.9

Harrison, Jane Ellen, 3, 4, 35, 37, 46–47, 48

Hathor, 117, 122, 168, 173–78

Hattusas, 168

Hawkes, Jacquetta, xvi

Hecate, 18, 45, 52, 96, 162, 198 n.8

Heket, 91, 94–96

Hellenistic culture, 115–17

Hephaistus, 40

Hera, 22, 42

Heracles, 104

Herefordshire, 139, *140*

Herm statues, 148–51, 153, 154

Herma (the word), 150

Hermes, 148, 150–52, 153, 155, 164–65

Herodotus, 26, 27, 36, 49, 115, 151, 175

Hesiod, 40, 106–7, 131

Hesychius of Alexandria, 4, 33

Hesychius of Miletus, 34, 153

Hetairai, 105

Hiera, 50

Hierophanies, 97

Hieros gamos, 5, 47, 48, 51

Hipparchus, 148, 150, 154, 198 n.6

Hippopotamus goddess, 96, 122, 174–75

Hittite deities, 167–72

Hocker posture, *xvi, xviii,* 87–91, 124, 137, 139

Homer, 125, 152

Homeric Hymns, 14

Homosexuality, 143

Horn symbolism, 67

Horus, 122, 176, 177

Humor (*see also* Laughter), 12, 16, 18, 39–40; in church iconography, 132; in *Great Contending*, 178; of Hermes, 152; *Inara and Telipinu* without, 172; in Thesmophoria festivals, 36–37

Hunting imagery, 59

Hymn to Demeter, xv, 13–17, 39–40, 50, 51, 52, 161–65; Demophoön in, 153; *Descent of Inanna* and, 172, 173; on Eleusinian Mysteries, 34; Hecate in, 198 n.8; *Hymn to Hermes* and, 151

"Hymn to Demeter" (Callimachus), 29–30, 33

Hymn to Hermes, 151, 198 n.6

Iacchus (*see also* Dionysus), 11, 22, 34, 153

Iambic meter, 15

Iambos (mythology), 48, 49

Iambos, (poetic form), 51

Ice Age iconography. *See* Paleolithic iconography

Illuminated manuscripts, 135–36, *137*, 138

Inanna, 172–73

Inara, 167–72

Indic iconography, 155–*58*

Indic rituals, 65

Indic women, 79, 103–4

Innocent VIII 144–45

Ino of Cadmus, 22

Inquisition, 130, 131, 144, 145

Inscriptions, 21–22, 50–51, 73, *75*, 151

Ion (Euripides), 109

Iraqi artifacts, *86*, 87

Irish ecclesiastical iconography, 139, 141, *142*, 143, 144

Iron Gate Gorge, 73

Ishtar, 47, 111

Isis, 3, 45, 47, 120, 126, 153; Apis and, *124*; Christianity and, 130–31; in Hellenistic Egyptian art, *9*, 117, *118–19*; witchcraft and, 122

Israeli artifacts, *76*, 77, 79

Italy, 116, 120, *132–33*, 135

Ithyphallic phallus, 148, 151, 154

Ivory artifacts, *66*, *71*, *82*, 95–96, 125

Japanese myth, 168, 179–81

Jesters, 18

Jesus Christ, 38

Jung, C. G., 52, 53, 54

Junker, Hermann (*see also* Pyramid Texts), 173

Ka gesture, 178

Kagura dance, 180

Kahin skirts, 182

Kalathos, 48, 51

Kali, 157

Kalinga women, 168, 181–85

Kamrupsepa, 171

Kedn' eiduia (the phrase), 13

Keleos, 18, 164

Kerenyi, Karl, 37, 51–52

Keuls, Eva, 41, 42, 104, 122

Khoiros (the word), 122, 195 n.11b

Kilpeck Church, 139, *140*, 143

Kiste, 48, 50, 51

Knives, 95–96

Kodiak Island, 125

Koilia, 4, 59, 177

Kojiki, 179
Kore. *See* Persephone
Korubas, 4
Kostenki, 67, *69*, 70
Koures, 4
Kteis, 49, 50
Kybele, 47, 50
Kykeon, *19*, 20, 34, 48, 51, 152, 163–64
Kyllene, Mount, 150

Ladder-of-the-soul, 120
Lagash, 22–24
Language of the Goddess (Gimbutas), 88, 125
Lascaux caves, 57
Laugerie Basse, 57, 65–*66*
Laughter (*see also* Humor), xix, 12, 39–40, 167, 180, 181
Laussel Venus figure, xvii, 66–*68*
Lepenski Vir, 73, *74*, *75*, 76–77
Lespugue figurine, 70–*72*
Libya, 108
Lilith, 139
Lincoln, Bruce, 52
Lingam, 156–57
Lotus symbolism, 96
Lucca Cathedral, 133, *133*
Lurker, Manfred, 45
Lycians, 184
Lygos plant, 38

Magic artifacts, *95*–96, 136–37, *138*
Magic lore, 152–53
Magnesia, 22
Maia, 150
Male actors, 12
Male artists, 103, 104, 105
Male dominance, xviii, 5, 11; in Athens,

41, 42, 104; Attic festivals and, 42, 43; in Judeo-Christian theology, 131
Male fears, 54, 111, 113
Male genitalia, 104–5, 135, 143, 148–51, 153–*55*, 156–57
Malleus Maleficarum, 144–45
M'alta figurine, 80, *82*, 83
Mammoth bone/ivory carvings, 65–*66*, 67, *69*, *71*, 80
Manuscript illumination, 135–36, *137*, *138*
Marble sculpture, 77, *80*–*81*
Marriage, 5, 47, 48, 51, 143
Marshack, Alexander, xvi, 63, 65, 66, 67, 83
Mary, Virgin, 18, 38, 79, 130
Matisse, Henri, 63
Mayauel, *xviii*
Meador, Betty De Shong, 37
Medes, 184
Medieval era, 96, 131–46
Medusa, 97, 105–13, *115*; in Athenian iconography, 148; in cathedral iconography, *132*–33; Evil Eye and, 125, *126*, 129; herms and, 150; Judeo-Christian theology and, 131, 135, 136; Psellus and, 35
Méduse (Claire), 111–13, 129
Megara, 31
Meheturt. *See* Hathor
Melian Gorgon/Medusa figure, 111, *112*
Mellaart, James, 10
Memphis, 26–27, 123–*24*
Menstruation (*see also* "Moon blood"), 37, 38–39, 67, 110, 171
Mercury, 153
Mermaid imagery, *133*, *134*, 135
Mesa Verde, 91

Mesopotamia, 22–24, 168

Metaneira, 18, 151, 163, 164

Michael Psellus, 3–4, 35–36

Midwives, 20

Miles, Margaret, 132

Mimbres people, 88, 91

Mimiambi (Herodas) 189 n.6

Minoan painting, *15*, 91, *92*

Mise, 18

Mithali, 103–4

Modena Cathedral, 135, *136*

Mogollen culture, 88

Mookerjee, Ajitcoomar, 157

"Moon blood," 5, 6, 38, 43, 110, 187 n.9

Moon cycles, 39, 67

Mother Goddess (*see also* Earth Mother), 63, 65, 155–56, 157, 169

Murray, Gilbert, 46

Murray, Margaret A., 47, 48; on Baubo, 24, 26, 27; on Isis, 45; on "Personified Yoni," 87; on Sheilahs, 139, 141, 143, 154

Das Mutterrecht (Bachofen), 46

Mylonas, George, 49–51, 101, 103

Myths, 97, 167, 173–74

Nakedness, 104–5, 131, 182–83

Native American iconography, 88, *89*

Naxos, 22, 51, 151

Necklaces, 77

Neith, 108

Neolithic iconography, 67, 70, 73–83, 91, 125

Nesteia, 37

Neumann, Erich, 85, 101, 120

New Mexico, 88

Nietzsche, Friedrich, 46

Nihongi, 179

Nile River, 120

Nîmes, 153–*54*

Ninshubur, 172–73

Nocturnal creatures, 18

Nubian Desert, 175

Nurses, 22

Obscenity, 5, 33, 36–37, 45, 49, 53

Old Corinth, 11, 12

"Old Europe," 10, 188 n.11

Old women, 96, 97

Olender, Maurice, 4–5, 8, 22, 48–49, 53, 96

Olympia, 42

Olympian pantheon, 16, 30, 101, 151, 165

Orpheus, 17

Orphic literature, 48, 49, 50, 51, 52; Hermes Chthonius in, 152; Iambe/Baubo in, 15, 17–20, 198 n.8

Orphism, 17

Osiris, 45

Oxford, 143

Paleolithic cosmology, 5–7

Paleolithic iconography, 55–70, 80, 83, *85*

Pan , 18

Pandora, 40–41, 129, 131

Paradise Lost (Milton), 96

Paros, 22, 51, 151

Parpan, Mariflor, 181, 182, 185, 200 n.19

Parvati, 157

Patriarchy. *See* Male dominance

Pegasus, 184

Pelasgians, 151

Perdrizet, Paul, 117, 120, 123, 124, 126

Persephone (*see also* Demeter-Persephone myth), 22, 38, 151

Perseus, *107*, 108, 110

Persians, 184

Petrie, Flinders, 47

Phaistos, 91, *92*

Phallocracy. *See* Male dominance

Phallus. *See* Male genitalia

Philippines, 168, 181–85

Philochorus, 18

Philosophy, 174

Phoenician deities, 24, 77, 78

Phrygian mythology, 18

Piacenza Cathedral, *132–33*

Picard, Charles: on Baubo, 47–48, 49;
    on "Baubo Upon a Sow," 120;
    Devereux and, 53; on Eleusinian cult,
    45, 49; on Greek genealogy, 17–18; on
    Priene Baubos, 101; on temple
    inscriptions, 22

Pigs, *121*, 122

Le Placard, 63, *64*, 65, 83

Plate drawing, 110, *112*

Plato, 105

Plutarch, 184

Polos, 115, 125

Pomegranate seeds, 37–38

Poseidon, 107, 184

Posture. *See* Body postures

Potnia Theron, 110

La Potta di Modena, 135, 136

Pottery painting (*see also* Vase painting),
    15, 86–87, 88, 89, 110, 111, 125–27

Praxiteles, 105

Priene Baubo statuettes, *100*, 101, *102*,
    103, 105, 115

Priene inscription, 22

*Prolegomena to the Study of Greek
    Religion* (Harrison), 3, 46–47

Prostitutes, 41, 135, 136, *137*

Psellus, Michael, 3–4, 35–36

Ptah, 27, 122–23

Puberty rites, 5, *10*, 37, 52–53

Pyramid Texts, 173, 175, 176

Ra-Atum, 174, 175, 176, 177, 178

Ramses VI, 178

Rawson, Philip S., 55, 57, 65

Rê, 174, 175, 176, 177, 178

"Records of Ancient Matters," 179

Reign of the Phallus (Keuls), 104

Reindeer bone carvings, 63, *64*, 65

Revelation. *See* Apocapypse

Rhea, 50

Rhodian Medusa plate, 110, *112*

Rice powder designs, 104

"The Ritual Baring of Hathor," 176–78

Roman Empire, 115, 117, 130

Roman mythology, 153

Romanesque churches, 132, 143

Ross, Anne, 141, 143

Ruck, Carl, 101

Russian nomads, 30

Russian Paleolithic iconography, 67, *69*,
    70

Sacred marriage, 5, 47, 48, 51

Saharan rock carvings, *85*

St. Domnēs festival, 20

St. Mary and St. David Church, 139, *140*

St. Michael Cathedral, 133, *133*

Salt, 59, *60*

Samuel, Abba, 136–37, *138*

San Pedro de Galligans, 133, *134*, 135

Sanday, Peggy Reeves, xviii, 147

Sardinian funerary customs, 18

Scandlach, 184–85

Scorpion imagery, 87, *88*

Scrolls, 136–37

Sculpture. *See* Marble sculpture; Stone carvings; Terra-cotta sculpture

Scythian gold ornaments, 115, *116*

Scythian nomads, 114–15

Seals, *xvi*, 87–88

Sekmet. *See* Hathor

Serapeum, 27

Servant figures, 151

Seth, 176, 177

Sexual antagonisms, xviii, 42, 79, 104, 105

Sexual organs. *See* Genitalia

Shameless Venus figure, 65–*66*

Shee (the word), 196 n.9

Sheilahs, 47, *140, 142,* 139–44, 154–*55*

Shelley, Percy Bysshe, 110

Shiva, 156–57

Shu, 175

Sicilian cup drawing, *126*

Sid (the word), 196 n.9

Sidon, 77

Sistrum, 120

Situla, 126

Sky gods, 30

Slavery, 41, 105

Soviet Paleolithic iconography, 65, 67, *69,* 70

Sow, *121,* 122

Spanish archeological sites, 57, *58*

Spanish ecclesiastical iconography, 133, *134,* 135–36, *137*

Spartan women, 41

Squatting posture, *xvi, xviii,* 87–91, 124, 137, 139

Srejović, Dragoslav, 73, 75

Stenno, 106

Stone, Merlin, 139

Stone carvings (*see also* Marble sculpture; Rock carvings), 153–54

Stone inscriptions, 21–22, 50–51, 73, *75,* 151

Sumerian deities, 22–24, *25, 86*–87, 111, 172–73

Sumerian women, 139

Susanowo, 168, 179, 180

Syracuse, 104

Syria, 24, 168

Taman Peninsula, 114, 115

Tantrism, 155–57

Taueret, 96, 122, 174–75

Tel Baiteglain, 79

Teletai, 33–34, 48, 103

Telipinu, 167–72

Tello, 25

Terra-cotta sculpture, 77, *78,* 117, *118*–22, 126–29

Textile crafts, 103, 104

Theater, 12, 39

Theban tomb paintings, *27*

Theodosius I, 35

Theogony (Hesiod), 106–7

Thesmophoria festivals, xv, 31, 36–39, 45, 51, 122; Baubo images and, 103; Egyptian worship and, 27, 29, 117

Thompson, William Irwin, 5–7, 39–40, 44, 67, 145–46

Thomson, George, 105

Thoth, 175, 176

Thracian mythology, 24

Tiâmat, 133

Toad symbolism, xiii, 18, 88–*95,* 96–97

Tomb offerings, 120

Tomb paintings, *27,* 115

Toulouse, 145

Trier Bishopric, 145

Triple Goddess, 108

Triptolemos, 17

Turkey, 168

Twins, 123

Ugarit, 24

Uma, 157

Underworld, 17, 152, 171

United Nations, 200 n.19

United States Southwest, 88, 91

Upraised arms, 84–86, 178

Ur, 87, *88*

Uzume, 168, 180

Vagina Dentata, 113, 131

Vase painting (*see also* Pottery painting);
    Athenian, 98, *99*, 101, 104–5;
    Eleusinian, *106*; Greek, *107*, *109*, *149*

Venus, xvii

Venus Impudique figure, 65–66

Venus of Galgenberg figure, *56*, 57, 59

Venus of Laussel figure, xvii, 66–68

Vervain bush, 38

Virgin Mary, 18, 38, 79, 130

Virgins (*see also* Brides; Chastity), 42, 135

Vivekananda, 157

Vulva (*see also* Vagina Dentata); in
    Eskimo rituals, 83; exposure of (See
    Ana-suromai); eye symbolism of, 126,
    127, 129; Gorgo symbolism of, 112–13;
    Greek terms for, 195–96 n.11b; in

Judeo-Christian theology, 131;
    Neolithic iconography of, 73, 77; in
    Paleolithic cosmology, 5–7;
    Paleolithic iconography of, *58–66*; pig
    symbolism of, 122; squatting posture
    and, 87; in Tantrism, *156*, 157

Walker, Barbara, 139

Walrus ivory carvings, 125

Water-snake goddesses, 133

Weddings, 143

Welsh ecclesiastical iconography, 139,
    144

Wet nurses, 22

Whittlesford, 154–55

"Wise blood," 171

Witchcraft, 47, 54, 96, 122, 131, 144–45

Woolf, Virginia, 157

Works and Days (Hesiod), 40

*Worship of the Generative Powers During
    the Middle Ages in Western Europe*
    (Wright), 139, 141

Wright, Thomas, 139, 141

Yoni, 87, *156*, 157

Zeus, 3; in Aegean inscriptions, 22, 151;
    Athena and, xvii, 108–9; in Demeter-
    Persephone myth, 11, 16, 161, 162, 164;
    in Eleusinian Mysteries, 4; Hermes
    and, 150, 151, 152; Pandora and, 40–41;
    Susanowo and, 180

THE METAMORPHOSIS OF BAUBO

was composed in 11.5 on 15 Adobe Garamond,

with display type in Lithos,

by Keystone Typesetting, Inc.;

printed on 60-pound Glatfelter Supple Opaque acid-free, recycled paper,

with 80-pound Rainbow Antique endsheets,

Smyth-sewn and bound over 88-point binder's boards

in Kingston Natural cloth,

or notch-bound in paperback,

by Thomson-Shore, Inc.;

with dustjackets and paperback covers printed in 3 colors

by Vanderbilt Printing Services.

Book and jacket design by Richard Hendel.

Published by Vanderbilt University Press,

Nashville, Tennessee 37235.